TRACKING SASQUATCH

GARY AND WENDY SWANSON

Unless otherwise credited, all images were provided from the files of Gary Swanson.

Cover Photo Image by Colourbox.com

Published by Swanson Literary Group
ISBN: 1985669633
ISBN-13: 978-1985669635

Other books by the authors:

They Saw Sasquatch
Bigfoot Uncovered
Sasquatch Encounters
SASQUATCH! Reports From the Field
Bigfoot Adventures
On the Trail of Sasquatch
Sasquatch is Out There
Squatchin': Study Guide and Field Handbook for Tracking Sasquatch
Hiking Sasquatch Country: Best Hikes In Southern Oregon

Skinwalkers Shapeshifters and Native American Curses
The Last Skinwalker
We Survived Native American Witches, Curses & Skinwalkers
Skinwalker: Guardian of the Last Portal

CONTENTS

INTRODUCTION

A "Bigfoot-sized" thank you to our growing list of friends who have contributed their stories of Sasquatch sightings and encounters!

You will notice that the contributors to this book are much more diverse in locations than our prior publications. Thanks to our audience interest, many stories have come from those who have held back from submitting their own experiences due to privacy concerns. We have proven our promise of secrecy, so more stories are arriving.

Some of our new stories came from this recent group and we can see how many of these folks have legitimate anxieties, and we will continue to provide complete anonymity for all who want it.

This book has a few surprises; probably our biggest revelation was from a gentleman who was as amazed as we when he finally opened his great grandfather's personal diary. He had left it unread for years, allowing for the sadness to lessen and when finally reading the hand written notes, he found himself following his great grandfather's encounters with Sasquatch, and the contact took place on, of all places, Oak Island, Nova Scotia!

You will read about Kiekhaefer Mercury Outboards secret test facility at "Lake X" in Florida and their resident Sasquatch.

Contributors from the upper Midwest areas of Michigan and Minnesota also reported their experiences. Mississippi managed to find room to add another "S" to its name, but this time it stands for Sasquatch!

Included are many exciting stories from a wide variety of Oregon residents and tourists in areas that the publishers know well. A surprising twist to Oregon's most outrageous city turned out to also involve members of a Sasquatch family; that city being none other than the infamous "Rajneeshpuram;" a commune of 18,000 worshippers who poisoned a city to sway an election!

Sasquatch played a big part in the adventures of modern day gold seekers in Oregon's coastal mountains and you can almost re-live some of these adventures enough to feel the intense fear when a soccer ball sized rock is thrown by a wild, hairy "mountain ape," as you're running for your life!

There is also a record of Sasquatch attacking a couple in a wilderness area in Utah and another one interrupting a vacation on a lake in Idaho.

You'll read about two Bigfoot encounters that took place in Northern California, where Sasquatch sightings take place almost as frequently as in Oregon.

I had cause to think back to my personal encounter when hiking in a Southern Oregon gold mining area when my recollection became clouded with doubt when my photo failed to accurately show what I knew I had seen, and further mental review allowed me to remove all further doubt and to officially declare that I had really seen Sasquatch!

A member of Oregon's senate once said to a good friend of mine, "Denny, I know what I saw; I was stone cold sober and there was this apelike being just 10 yards away, facing me. Those reddish-yellow eyes seemed like they were reading my mind, and then it turned and in five seconds, I couldn't even hear it running anymore. This was a moment so exciting to me, and so amazing I want to tell the world, but I can't because I'd never get reelected again!"

I and so many more people feel the same way, but until proof is at hand, at least we are among very credible friends!

We hope that you will enjoy the reports as much as we have, and we can take comfort in the fact that not everything has been discovered, so there are still roads untraveled for us all to take!

If you have had a personal encounter or sighting of a Sasquatch that you would like to see published in our next book, please send the details and any accompanying photos to:

swanliterary@gmail.com

If your story is published you will receive a copy of the book as our thanks.

ALL THE BELLS AND WHISTLES

A few words of caution from our contributors: Many of our writers warn of the dangers of trying to photograph or at least enjoy the experience of meeting a Sasquatch.

Remember that these are wild animals and should be kept at a safe distance. Many of our contributors say the safe place to stop is the minute you see one.

Cougars and wolves are growing in population, and bears are always a danger. Never come between an animal and its young; no matter what species!

Many of those hiking our more wild regions suggest wearing small bells and carrying whistles to chase off threats.

Here's where having all the "Bells and Whistles" comes in handy. Hikers are advised to be cautious around rivers and streams, and not to reach into holes without first probing with a stick, although rattlers will normally sense vibration and move off.

Bears and cougars will use the same trails you do, and it's helpful to be able to recognize their scat. Bear droppings will have an abundance of fur and berries and cougar scat will contain animal fur, and also small "bells and whistles." Just kidding; have fun and stay safe!

Be prepared by bringing plenty of water for each member of your party. You should also bring some extra high energy snacks, a first aid kit, and yes, a whistle. It's not a good idea to hike alone in rugged country. If you are hiking with dogs, don't forget to bring plenty of water and snacks for them as well.

Know where you are going, and make sure someone else knows where you are going to be and when you plan to return. Be sure to have a good map of the area, because you cannot always rely on GPS systems. People have died in wilderness areas by trusting only their GPS, as mountains can affect their functioning.

Respect the environment, whatever you pack in; make sure you take it back out. You will not find any trash barrels or bathroom facilities along the way!

1 OAK ISLAND SASQUATCH

I was recovering at home from a broken leg, and my wife Patty suggested that now would be a good time to go through the old steamer trunk left to me when my last living relative was gone. I had been avoiding doing this for several years, but I knew I couldn't put if off any longer. Having tried this once before, I had quit when it became too tearful, as I had lost all contact for so many years. It seemed as if a major part of my life had gone on without me.

While Patty kept me supplied with snacks and beverages, I made pretty fast work of the old newspapers and family photos; the majority of the latter, showing people I couldn't remember; and then I found the old diary!

It had been handed down from my great grandfather who was born into the family's business of the manufacture of military weaponry and munitions. Most of the diary's entries were rather mundane when describing the details of his duties and details of his daily life, until I came upon a notation that just stood out like it was in lights!

The comment began, "Heading out for a couple of days with some friends to Smith's Island," and then he had drawn a line through "Smith's" and written, "Guess I should be calling it Oak Island now since the cartographer made the latest change before they started selling lots again."

I never would have paid the inked out name any attention had I not watched the television program on the "Oak Island" treasure hunt a couple of days before. I yelled out for Patty to come in, and we both sat stunned as searching on her laptop revealed that Oak Island had indeed gone through various name changes due to multiple owners, cartographer's whims and property owners disputing each other's choices. Add to this discovery, the fact that Grandfather was born in Halifax, Nova Scotia, and it was indisputable truth that my great grandfather had actually camped on that same Oak Island!

Now Patty and I were reading the diary together. Great Grandfather made detailed comments of their campsite, and he elaborated enough that we had the feeling that relaxation such as this came seldom back in those times. Then things changed!

Oak Island, Nova Scotia – 1931
By Pacific Southwest Region U.S. Fish and Wildlife Service, photographer unknown [CC BY 2.0 (http://creativecommons.org/licenses/by/2.0) or Public domain], via Wikimedia Commons

The next observations were written so we could almost feel the tension he was experiencing as he referred to "two large and gangly haired bush apes." He went on to say, "These Sasquatch apes were down beside the skiff and trying to tear it loose from the mooring when we came running down the sloping bank yelling and throwing rocks. The distance to shore was about 200 metres, and these Yeti creatures swam it in only a couple of minutes, and although we had seen many of them before, none of us knew they could swim. Then we saw their secret; they had been hanging on to a short piece of log; of which the waters in the area were virtually littered with from all of the timber harvesting operations." After a short description of the rest of his rather normal outing, it ended.

That was my great grandfather's last entry, as a few days later he was killed along with over 2,000 other people on December 6, 1917 when the French ammunition ship, SS Mont Blanc, collided with SS Imo, a Norwegian steamship, in Halifax harbor!

Norwegian Steamship SS Imo aground on Dartmouth shore after the Halifax explosion – 1918
By Nova Scotia Archives and Records Management – public domain

The large diary also contained several old photographs that were glued on the pages, and there was Great Granddad in a photo earlier in 1917 seated beside Franklin Delano Roosevelt with the notation; "Pact meeting with Franklin D. Roosevelt, Assistant Secretary of the U. S. Navy." All this time I had never known anything about my great grandfather, and here he was with my nine year-old grandfather sitting on his lap beside the future president of the United States of America! Turning the page, I saw that my grandfather had a note on the page saying that he wished to honor his father by "continuing to use this diary to record family history." Then with the world war and the family's company in the munitions business, the diary must have sat awhile before he made any further entries.

Judging from the dates, Grandfather Roland must have waited for a fair number of years before he began recording his own follow-up, of which I was perusing the rather mundane record of his weekly activities, when my eyes again focused on the words "Oak Island." There was Grandfather's notation, "Had a run-in with one of those 'Buckwus' or 'Sasquatch' apes today. They seem to come out of the deep woods at dusk and hunt. Don't know all what they eat, but fruit for sure, and potatoes. Farmers around here are losing some small critters like cats, goats and sheep. I met one near Smith's Cove on my very rare time off, so I was not prepared to give way. A few shouts and waving of fists, coupled with it being smaller than I, caused it to lurch off into the woods. Constable Carruthers and our game management team will hold a meeting to study this increasing problem, and an attempt to study this creature will be discussed with the CCCWP." I later looked up this abbreviation Grandfather made, and learned it stood for the Cross Canadian Council for Wildlife Protection.

That was Grandfather's last note, and the book became a casualty with no further entries. My father evidently had decided not to continue the family records, but this was part of my family that I found too late to have anyone left to ask questions of. Guess I'll never know.

Josiah Winthorpe ~ Fredericton, New Brunswick, Canada

2 LOOK BEHIND YOU

Publishers note: This letter came in three months after the first reported encounter was received, and since they are both from Nova Scotia, we placed them close together for their kinfolk; who may know each other.

I grew up in Bangor, Maine, and my father was a junior partner in the sporting goods business. I cannot mention the company, because my dad's retirement clause prohibits use of the name. I'll simply say that father had worked for the same company since he graduated from college, so there were a lot of perks. I mention this only to say that our family benefited from those bonuses; myself probably more than the rest, even though I am a female. Since my brother had joined one of the major auto manufacturing corporations in the United States, I happily filled the spot that normally would have been for a male in the corporate succession ladder. I soon realized that being a "girl," I was a token figure primarily useful for public relations, although I doubt I was taken as seriously as a man would have been.

I purely loved travelling with Father, as I was introduced to some of the most terrific sporting personalities in the world! Over a period of several summers prior to entering college, I attended what were known as "high level" meetings where my opinion was often sought so as to represent the company's fast growing product segment that catered to the female sportsperson.

My big break came during my second year of college, as the company was opening several more franchises in Canada, and they made me an offer, thanks to Dad's influence I admit, but I will also admit to being a perfect fit for the position. This was too good an opportunity, so I took a break from school, so that I could see what would be required knowledge for my new position when I continued my schooling, which the company offered to pay for!

My first assignment was to move to Halifax, Nova Scotia, and my fellow employees were marvelous. They took me under their wings like a member of their family, and I assimilated quickly. The company had taken my advice, and closed the deal for our newest franchise, so my job now was to totally devote my time to ensure that we gave our full support to the success of this brand new location.

I know I'm rambling, but the memories of those days are so rewarding that I get caught up, so let me get to my experience with the scariest animal I've ever seen!

Several of us employees began to bond soon after we first met, and before long, we were a close circle of eight people with similar interests. Our main organizer, Paul, had been with this group for a long time before they became our franchise, and being the newcomer to the team, I was satisfied to merely be a part of the fun. Before long, we had narrowed down to an almost inseparable six people; we had many common interests, but our main hobby was sailing.

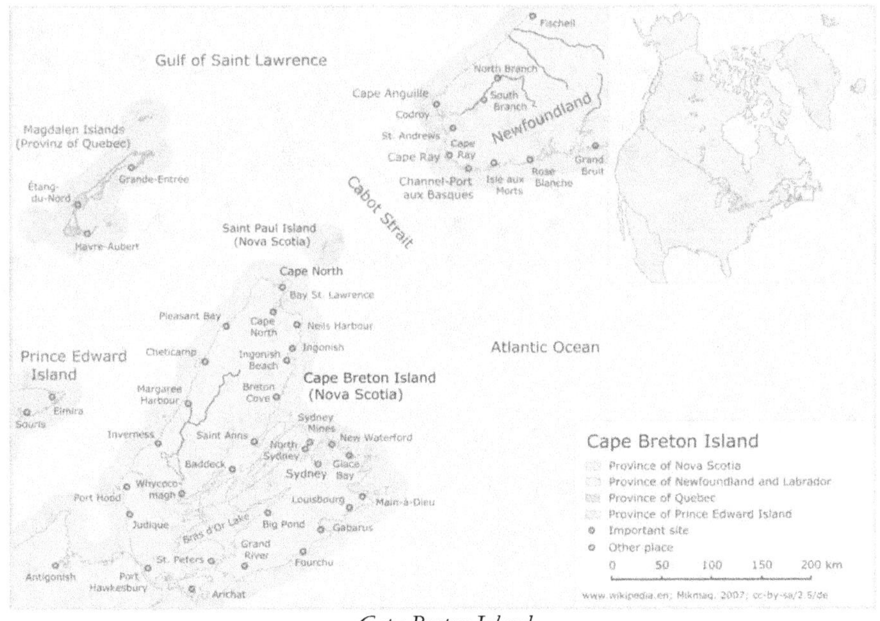

Cape Breton Island
By Klaus M. (Image (Map) made by Klaus M. (Mikmaq), Germany) [CC BY-SA 2.5
(https://creativecommons.org/licenses/by-sa/2.5)], via Wikimedia Commons

Here's where I finally get my story out! I heard from a friend that you had a Facebook page where people can submit a Bigfoot story, and I have a story that I hope you will include in your next book. I have procrastinated long enough, because my story actually happened back in 2007 on a boating jaunt, on my friend Jeannie's father's yacht.

Her dad took us on a four day trip from his moorage in Dartmouth, and we met a business associate from Sydney at Port Hawkesbury, which was a point between where they were purchasing a piece of land at the port facility.

Jeannie and I hung around on the yacht, and the second day, we were headed back toward Halifax when Jeannie's dad got a call from a real estate developer saying he wanted to meet him at Mahone Bay to discuss a real estate development at, Oak Island.

Mahone Bay
By Graham-H (Pixabay)

Back then, this place had not received the notoriety it has today. It was just a small island off the coast near Lunenburg. Sure, we knew that the place had been the topic of a lot of stories about pirate treasure and strange happenings, and I hadn't lived in that area long enough to learn much about it, but also, I had zero interest in exploring for old coins and digging in holes where snakes lived!

Anyway, we soon dropped anchor off a small island about 600 to 1000 feet from the shore. There was a small marina like area on the mainland, with a parking lot for vehicles and docks evidently for visitors and the people who had homes that I could see the roofs of, as the island was higher than our deck. Jeannie and I didn't pay much attention as a small power boat picked up her dad and left for

Oak Island. One of his crewmen went along and the other two remained on the boat with us.

We were swaying slightly and the anchor rope had enough play in it that soon we were floating close enough to get a clear look at the shoreline. The ship's binoculars certainly made for closeups of the flags and stakes where the lots for sale were stretched out from the house and some other building of which we could only see a roof, because of the island's height.

I think I must have been watching long enough to have been half asleep when I became aware of an animal moving in the overgrown weeds down along the shore. I looked over at Jeannie, and she was slumped over, sound asleep. I shook her awake and whispered for her to look; and as she turned to where I was pointing, another much bigger animal joined the first one. They just stood there eating berries from the bushes. I assumed them to be raspberries, or similar, but I suddenly woke up enough to realize that I was not looking at an animal I was familiar with!

These were not normal wildlife. Jeannie finally broke from her trancelike state, and as she turned to me, she said, "Sasquatch!" As we both watched through our binoculars, the animals didn't seem as though they were even aware of our being there; of course, the ever present wind blew constantly across this vast waterway. Then, as we were staring open-mouthed, Jeannie's dad came over the hill with the other man and his crewman. Her dad and the man in the suit shook hands, and the man went back up the hill as her dad returned to the boat. He was soon at the yacht, and as the boat was raised to its sling, we regaled her dad on the animals we had been watching.

Jeannie's dad joined us on the deck, and as he was served a scotch by his white frocked crewman, he settled into a lounge chair as we continued our story. When we finally ran out of breath, her dad filled me in on why he hadn't thought to tell me that I may see one of these Sasquatch. He said the locals accepted them, and seldom had there been any problems with the big animals. They never had any confrontations, because the beasts seemed terrified when coming upon people, but they weren't scared enough to stay away when the berries were ripe. The locals kept silent about the Sasquatch because they were known to be in several better publicized areas nearby and the islander's didn't want the trespassers and their cameras anywhere near. As our boat powered away, I took one last look back, but there was not a sign of the creatures. Evidently there were a great number of areas in that wild country where colonies of them lived all year round in harmony with the local people.

Lily ~ Bangor, Maine

3 THE MUD CREEK SASQUATCH

Finally, I saw my first Sasquatch! I have many friends who have been telling me about seeing these animals for several years now, but I had never had a glimpse of one until a drizzly day last spring.

Moose Lake, Minnesota Moose Statue
By Nielseno [GFDL (http://www.gnu.org/copyleft/fdl.html), CC-BY-SA-3.0
(http://creativecommons.org/licenses/by-sa/3.0/) or CC BY-SA 2.5-2.0-1.0
(https://creativecommons.org/licenses/by-sa/2.5-2.0-1.0)], via Wikimedia Commons

I had been out east of my hometown of Moose Lake in Northern Minnesota shooting in a gravel pit on Mud Creek Road. The pit hadn't been used since I don't know when; I can't disclose the exact location, as I have friends who maintain a private "garden" in the vicinity. I had been shooting cans, rocks, and "missing" a few mud turtles. In my defense, their little heads are hard to see when they peek up from the water.

This particular area required high rubber boots if one doesn't wish to spend the day with wet feet. I had been walking along a peat bog, which if you are familiar with them, is like trying to walk through a huge, wet swamp with grass about two to three feet high, and every couple of steps you have to balance on a grass hummock. It's like trying to navigate a monstrous gymnasium filled with a thousand "My Pillows!" Up and down and over, and the entire time, I was also fighting my way through a very dense and massive plain of willow trees, whose branches were constantly whipping my face and arms, and had I not been on a path leading to higher ground, I'd have gone home after the first 20 minutes of torture.

Finally I reached dry land, and I climbed the side of the old gravel pit and over the berm to an area of paper targets, cans, bottles, PVC pipe, and a carpet of empty shotgun shells; and everywhere, there was the mess and trash that makes a target shooter feel right at home. This pit, at one time, had been used for many projects, and my father had told me it had been used by a railroad called the "Soo Line," of which the railroad bed still exists in the area.

The last trip of Soo Line 2719 in its excursion career before the mandated FRA rebuild By KAM32296 (Own work) [CC BY-SA 3.0 (https://creativecommons.org/licenses/by-sa/3.0)], via Wikimedia Commons

The sun finally reminded me of its presence, and I sat down on a grass covered, clay bank to have the small lunch I had brought, and allow my boots and pants to dry out. After a while, I searched around and found remnants of cans, partial bottles and a pail, and I created several targets that would keep me entertained for a time.

I knew that there was no danger of ricochet, as my backdrop was a dirt bank that was about 20 feet high. So I cut loose in a session of rapid fire until my .22 caliber pistol ran dry. As the slide locked open on the last round, a rock came from my right and almost hit me in the head! I likely wouldn't have even seen it, had it not been for it being slightly preceded by a loud screech!

The shriek scared me more than the rock that missed, because it hit my ears. I turned to my right as my left hand had pulled out a spare magazine, and I reloaded as I came face to face with my attacker. Not a close face to face or I'd have messed myself; and I ran for my life, but as I looked back, staring after me was a very angry ape! It was a big monster that seemed over 12 feet tall, but as scared as I was (I freely admit it), I believe it was more like six feet tall with another six feet of my fear. I was truly in shock!

I had often been told by my friends who spent time in these swampy areas that these Sasquatch were real, but until I actually met one, I just figured they might have been shaggy wolves from the newly introduced pack in our area by the federal government.

I'd like to say I tried to communicate with it, or at least tried to study it from a distance, but to be perfectly honest, I felt my life was in danger at that very moment, and it wasn't until after I got back to my rig and was back in Moose Lake that my butt stopped puckering.

I only dared share this story with a couple of friends, but to protect their secrets, I cannot disclose the exact location.

Tommy T. ~ Moose Lake, Minnesota

4 BIGFOOT OF WOLF CREEK

A relative of mine had been a sort of "partner" in the Wolf Creek Inn* near Grants Pass, Oregon, which is on current Interstate Highway 5. I will not give her name, as her descendants, including myself, are still, after all these years, at odds over disputed claims on a fair-sized sum of money and land ownership.

Back in the waning years of stagecoach travel and the building of the railroad, there was a period where both services were using the same stopovers, and there was a tent city on the grounds surrounding the Wolf Creek Inn to house the railroad crews.

Wolf Creek Inn, Josephine County, Oregon

Workers would pick up lunches from the kitchen, and evening meals were served inside the main hall and in large mess tents. These railroad laborers worked hard and there was very little partying, drinking, gambling, or even fighting at night after the long work shifts.

The rooms in the Inn were occupied by regular stagecoach passengers and the occasional railroad executive, but the top brass usually had Pullman coaches on sidings next to the track laying, so as to not only save expenses, but to allow the inns along the way to earn an uninterrupted living from regular travelers who depended on their accommodations, as in those days, you couldn't just drive down the line to the next hotel.

Well, according to Aunt Emily's notations in her diary, there were several incidents that she had to respond to; such as visitations by a large ape-like creature that at first was described as a bear that walked on its hind legs. Emily's notes in her diary on several pages showed that the majority of the people back then had absolutely no knowledge of apes, gorillas, and other creatures, as America's vast western areas were still in "pioneer mode," and for the most part, only familiar with animals common to their own environment. Occasionally schools would show drawings of exotic animals from other areas, but seldom would parents have exposure to their offspring's primers, and if so, the fathers seldom had the luxury of even glancing at the drawings, as simply surviving was an effort in those tough times!

Aunt Emily made notes on maybe one out of every four or five pages about these large, hairy and man-like "giant bears" that walked on their hind legs and used their oversized, hairy paws like humans do.

Several of the tracklayers who were in the capacity of today's foremen, carried revolvers; and my aunt cited several instances where there had been shots fired at these giants, but she didn't indicate if any were killed or wounded; however, the many notations she had related, would indicate that they were important enough events to cause everyone concern at the time.

There would be stretches of time where Aunt Emily didn't make any notations, so it wasn't like a "dear diary" book; it was more of a record of events that were worth noting.

Only one encounter seemed important enough to have many notations on various search parties or "posses" as my aunt called them such at the time, where about 30 men went armed to the small, rough mountain that has since been renamed "London Peak" in pursuit of two of these animals that had totally destroyed one of only two mercantile and food supply stores in the area. Although Aunt Em noted that a lot of food had been apparently eaten, there were opened sacks of flour and sugar that showed tracks of multiple animals that she noted looked like four or five adults, but maybe two smaller ones as well.

Em noted, after a mob pursued the group toward what is now "London Peak," many shots were reportedly fired and the men claimed to have killed at least two of them, but they said the animals were way up on the steep cliffs, and after they fell, no bodies were ever found. Believe me though, those steep, jagged cliffs could hide clouds!

View of I-5 from London Peak Scenic Overlook, May 2, 2017
By Greg Shine, BLM

I have not been in that area for many years, but I have an uncle who lives in Roseburg, Oregon, which is only a few miles away, and he said his father was in that posse, so he verified that part of it as factual. He also said that many of his relatives still living in Wolf Creek have often spoken of what they called the "Wolfmen of Wolf Creek!" No, that wasn't where the name came from; just a later nickname according to other "old timers" I have spoken with.

J. D. Wallerman, Sr. ~ Oregon

Publishers note: The Wolf Creek Inn in Southern Oregon has a long history, and even Sasquatch seems to have visited here. The Wolf Creek Inn was a major stagecoach stop and was a favorite vacation spot for Clark Gable and Carole Lombard. Jack London spent months here writing his best-selling novel, "Valley Of The Moon." Prior to that, the Inn was visited regularly by the stagecoach driven by "One Eyed" Charley Parkhurst, who was once held up by the legendary bandit, "Black Bart!"

"One-eyed" Charley Parkhurst was one of Wells Fargo's best and most well-known stagecoach drivers. Charley was a rough-spoken, tobacco chewing, cigar smoking, and card playing individual. Although sociable,

Charley preferred sleeping in the stables with the horses rather than sharing quarters with the other drivers.

It wasn't until Charley Parkhurst died in 1879 that people discovered Charley was actually a woman. "Charlotte Parkhurst" was born in 1812 in Vermont, the same year that her mother died. Sometime prior to 1817 her father dropped her off at a New Hampshire orphanage. She later escaped from the orphanage by wearing boys' clothing, and found work in a livery stable. She eventually made her way west, working in stables along the way.

By Wikicuda (Own work) [CC BY-SA 4.0 (https://creativecommons.org/licenses/by-sa/4.0)], via Wikimedia Commons

She stayed in California after retiring from driving. It was here that she cast a ballot in the 1868 Presidential election; perhaps making her the first woman to vote in the United States. So, did she vote for Hyrum Ulysses Grant or Horatio Seymour?

5 COVINGTON COUNTY SASQUATCH

My first Sasquatch encounter takes place at my grandparents' farm in Collins, Mississippi. The property has been owned by my family for generations going back to my great grandfather. Lord knows how long this has been going on around here; perhaps people just didn't talk about it for whatever reasons. When my grandfather passed in mid-2008, I moved in with my grandmother to help take care of things that she wasn't able to do, and shortly after is when I really started to notice curious things.

First, there were sounds like someone slapping the house; and very loudly at that. The thing is, I trimmed all the tree branches back years prior and kept them that way, so I know it wasn't that causing the noise. The slapping was so loud, my grandmother who was very hard of hearing, even with hearing aids, was awakened one night by the sounds.

There were other nights as I was lying in bed, rolled over on my side, looking between the gap between the window shade and the side of the window and I saw a great big head and very broad shoulders at the top of the window. The width of this creature was far wider than any man or woman.

To help you picture the house, it is about a hundred years old, and is on a block foundation about a foot or so off the ground. The ceilings are quite high, maybe nine to ten feet, and the windows are about six feet tall themselves. I have spent many hours trying to figure out exactly what I saw outside my window that night.

Another encounter I had happened in December of 2011. I was out hunting on the back of our property. We have around 375 acres, and part of it is surrounded by nothing but woods and a creek on the back side; there was plenty of wildlife going through this area. It was late, about nine or a little before. The skies were overcast, but it was a full moon and it poked through from time to time. I exited my stand and started up a small hill to look out over the rest of the pasture that was perhaps 75 yards from my stand when I got this feeling of being watched. I spun around with my flashlight and I saw two eyes maybe 25 to 30 yards from me; the being was standing there glaring at what seconds before was my back. It didn't run away like most animals do. My first thought was who is back here with me? So I called out and got a grunt in return. By this time the clouds broke and lit it up; yeah that was the fastest I ever made that mile to the house on foot! I knew right then what it was; a Bigfoot. As I was leaving, it picked up a tree branch and gave a wood knock.

I have always heard sounds on my grandparents' property that weren't quite animal. They were almost human sounding, but not a panther or bobcat.

Remnant of a cypress/tupelo wetland in an oxbow in central Mississippi
Lynn Betts / Photo courtesy of USDA Natural Resources Conservation Service., via Wikimedia
Commons

The most alarming encounter happened in 2015 just south of my grandparents place when I was house-sitting for a friend. Her back door was in the living room and you could see it as you were watching TV. She had a dog door installed in the door so her dogs and one roaming cat could come in and out.

So I am sitting there one night; it was getting late, around 9:00 p.m. or so. The cat strolls by and into the kitchen, and about 15 minutes later I see something playing with the dog door from the outside; I knew it wasn't my dog because he was sitting by me and was acting a little set back by whatever the scent was he had just picked up. Of course I naturally thought I missed seeing the cat go out. Keep in mind; this is a single wide trailer house. You walk into the living room from either door; from the front door the kitchen and master bed room are to your left and the back door and other two rooms to your right.

I got up to go mess with the cat, and looked to my left into the kitchen, and guess who's in there looking at me? The cat! So then I thought it was another cat or a coon, since the house is set out in the middle of nowhere. So I ease over to the door, put my back against the wall and wait for the little varmint to push in the dog door again. Yeah, it wasn't a little critter at all. What came through the dog door was a huge, hairy hand; bigger than I have ever seen, kind of black in color. I hollered out, and the hand disappeared. As you can imagine, I didn't go to sleep that night!

The last story is back at my grandparents this year (2017), the weekend of Thanksgiving. Keep in mind, my grandfather kept cows and my uncles now do. Also, about a hundred yards from the house is a holding pen. It was dark and with no lights down there, so I couldn't see anything, but I could hear very well. I stepped out to what sounded like a man grunting very loudly for about a minute. It stopped, but I didn't see anyone leave; no lights moving or anything; and the highway runs right along the property line, so I know no one went out to the highway or through the pasture or woods with any type of light.

Those are my stories and I am sticking to them.

Bryan Blake ~ Collins, Mississippi

6 KILLING SASQUATCH

Back in 1983, my girlfriend and I joined friends who had become affiliated with the thousands of people living in the spiritual commune of Rajneeshpuram* in Central Oregon. We dropped out of school in Southern California and on recommendations from friends, made the trip into the craziest adventure one could ever imagine!

I have long wanted to confess my guilt, but since my life at that time was so screwed up, I hardly knew if it was reality or just a bad dream! Having read your Facebook page and reading your submitters' feedback, I am sending you this story with your assurance of absolute confidentiality. I must have your promise of complete secrecy, as I have changed my life totally, as now I am married with children and have a great job. Maybe those poor animals that died will have some rest now. I know this sounds melodramatic, because I actually never saw them buried, but I was told they were burned! Those days were all so hazy, it seemed like I was continually in a fog. I think we all were; all 18,000 "pot smoking rebels!"

When we arrived at this place in the middle of the high desert in Oregon, we were flabbergasted! There, in the most desolate place we had ever seen, was a paved airport with the same DC-3s, or similar to the plane type we had flown from L.A. to Portland on. We arrived at a modern, certified airport with several large planes, a helicopter, a newly built terminal, and paved runway; complete with lights, tower and the works; in the middle of nowhere! Plus that it was certified by the FFA as a legitimate, legal airport.

We entered the city of Rajneeshpuram expecting to see a bunch of scraggly tents and tepees, but instead, we were greeted by a friendly group of polite members of the welcoming committee; who fed us, assigned guest quarters to us, offered all the free pot we wished to smoke, and after only a day as guests, we gladly attended their indoctrination in the huge meditation and speech hall along with at least one or two thousand other recently arrived indoctrinees. It was easy to tell who the permanent residents were, because they were all wearing red clothing. They weren't uniforms, but all configurations and with wooden beads around their necks.

Meditation and Speech Hall in Rajneeshpuram
SAMVADO Gunnar Kossatz [CC BY-SA 2.0 de (https://creativecommons.org/licenses/by-sa/2.0/de/deed.en)], via Wikimedia Commons

Everything about the place seemed perfect for us, because the entire, stressed-out world had just been left behind, and here among around 15,000 permanent residents; we were accepted for who we appeared to be, with no other qualifications other than to join the others in building our own city with our own culture. Money seemed plentiful, and we soon found out this commune had unlimited cash on hand! The housing varied from wood built Quonset type A-frames, to traditional nice homes; all new, except for buildings from the former "Big Muddy Ranch."

We immediately accepted the few rules, and with full realization that we were expected to work alongside the other residents to build our community into a successful venture. There was not to be a larger or loftier goal, and there were no real days off. Everyone was expected to participate, and although the wages were low, everything was provided; and like I said, we had a massive pot farm, so the smoke was free and unlimited!

There we were in our red outfits, and there seemed to be no limit to the money behind this project. There was all the heavy equipment one could imagine, and residents learned how to operate it from the companies they purchased it from. We were encouraged to learn how to drive bulldozers, backhoes and tractors, and use chainsaws, and all sorts of equipment. We all shared what we had learned with each other. Where experts were needed to instruct us in other areas, they were hired; and for paving projects such as streets, roads, home construction, roofing and concrete projects, it was all hired from outside contractors. Elaborate water and sewer systems were already in the ground. Commune, hell; this was a town!

My curiosity grew when I saw the millions of dollars in expenditures, and it was explained that the Bhagwan had many wealthy donors. To indicate that point more was the fact that Bhagwan Shree Rajneesh owned a fleet of 84 Rolls Royce automobiles, all registered to him and his corporation, and with clear titles! One of our closest friends with whom we became really connected with, told us these were gifts from his contributors from across the U.S.A. and other countries.

We met our first Sasquatch when a group of us were assigned to a clandestine project, which was to plant around a thousand trees and shrubs to camouflage our very secret crematorium. This was "off limits" for questions and it took a month before we even learned what we were concealing!

After working for hours, we took a break and while were eating our sandwiches in a grassy area, we saw a large, furry animal in the back of the truck bed. It was squatting there and the lid was open on our cooler. Then we saw another one rummaging in the cab, so we all yelled out, and the two animals ran quickly into the brush. A supervisor happened by and we told him what happened, and he apologized for not warning us in advance, but no harm was done. We weren't too shook up over the event as no one was hurt, and we were curious when others came up and questioned us as to where we met the Sasquatch and where they went after that.

No more was said until a couple of days later when about an hour after dusk we heard a lot of shooting back in the woods where we had been working. Someone said that it sounded like a machine gun, and one of the camp directors overheard him and came over. He told us to forget about what we had heard; that it was probably "security" checking their weapons. They had a huge security force that was more like an army unit.

Inquiring of a few friends the next day, we found out that our security force was a lot bigger than we had thought. We were told that there were over 300 security people on the police force, and supposedly another 200 more who were considered deputies who were armed at all times! Further inquiries proved that we did hear fully automatic shooting, and that all security people had Uzi 9mm weapons with folding butt stocks and 30 round magazines. In addition to them, we were told with no particular caution, that over 2,000 more "sannyasins" had at least one, and some had as many as six firearms in their residences! This was a heavily armed camp; we learned that permanent residents numbered 12 to 15 thousand or more!

One of our friends leaned in our A-frame one afternoon, and quietly mentioned something like, "There's more to this place than meets the eye. Just be careful not to ask too many questions, but remember, this is all for all of our safety. Even the state and county law enforcement know that we take care of our own security, and they do not expect to protect us regardless of what happens!" That was why the day the Wasco County sheriff came to arrest one of our guests for a crime he committed in The Dalles, they didn't even question why at least 30 of our people were openly carrying guns.

When the four of us "landscapers" arrived at our planting site the next day, we saw a bunch of crows flying all around the edge of our work area calling and scolding loudly. When we investigated, we found two of the big Sasquatch animals all bloody and shot to pieces! (Note: Shortly after we got on our work detail, the supervisor had told us that we may see some large, hairy, chimpanzee-like animals, and that there was a small colony that lived back in a valley.) Before we could get over our shock, two Chevy Blazers full of security people came tearing up and they stopped in a huge cloud of dust and told us to leave the area immediately. We left and returned to the townsite for a beer. A while later, two security men appeared and pulled up chairs alongside us and very quietly asked us if, "…we had any problem with what we had seen?" We told them no, and they just said, "Good; keep it that way;" then they got up and left!

We later found out that this was not the first time something like this had happened, and one of the residents explained to us that they regularly had heard reports about the security force being more like the Gestapo. Word was that all rule-breakers and other crimes were "tried" by our own court system. We were cautioned to be very careful, because no outside authorities ever got involved and all crimes committed at Rajneeshpuram were tried and punished here!

While we lived among these people, everything was very harmonious, our personal pay increased, and it was a very comfortable existence; although there seemed no other benefits, like jobs that paid wages to be accumulated for retirement or anything for the future. Everyone except the higher-ups like the Bhagwan or Ma Anand Sheela were living "day to day" as we were. No responsibilities, no liabilities, just a no pressure, no obligation life of simply "being." When you're high on pot, that seems to be all one could ask for!

We have always regretted the murder of those Sasquatch! We had never seen such creatures before, and knowing they were viciously murdered for someone's "sport" is inconceivable! I guess these creators of their own empire acted like gods because those in charge of this city really seemed to believe they were immortal, the way they acted. I guess that's what comes from "smokin' what they were growin'." The Bhagwan seemed to float around in his own world without a care besides prayer and driving fast on his private highway.

Now all four of us were beginning to tire of the way the camp was beginning to fill with more and more freeloaders; whom we found out were being brought in to vote in the upcoming elections. The security people began to act like prison guards, so one day we took the community bus into The Dalles, Oregon and then we caught a shuttle to Portland and went back to California. We finally grew up after living for eight months without a care in the world; it had its limitations.

This is the first time we have told anyone about the killings of those Sasquatch, but the event still haunts us to this day!

Anonymous ~ Southern California

Publishers note; Rajneeshpuram explained: Gary Swanson was a resident of Portland, Oregon back when the Rajneesh was building his commune and he remembers seeing the red-clad residents walking on some dirt roads as he traveled through the areas around The Dalles; he never ventured into the city itself, but he can recall how much of the news reports were dominated by the Rajneeshees' activities.

Oregon Route 218 entering Antelope from the northwest
By Ian Poellet (Own work) [CC BY-SA 4.0 (https://creativecommons.org/licenses/by-sa/4.0)], via Wikimedia Commons

A major reason the commune was forced out was when they tried to fraudulently win the Wasco County, Oregon election. Since no love was lost between the elected officials in Wasco County and the Bhagwan Shree

Rajneesh and his people, the county officials planned to openly pass laws as soon as the election was over that would virtually force the Rajneeshees to shut down.

So the word went out that all street people of voting age were welcome at Rajneeshpuram; they were offered free room and board, and all the weed they could smoke; a pothead's dream!

The city was bringing in Portland's street people by the bus load. Many of the people that were arriving were direct from Los Angeles. Word was out, and Rajneeshpuram now looked like it could completely dominate the polls in the upcoming election. They thought it was in the bag until a previously unknown residency requirement of six months surfaced through intensive research by Wasco County and state officials as they feverishly looked for loopholes!

The Rajneeshees acted fast, as they wanted to get rid of all evidence of trying to rig the election. Also, since they now had several thousand unnecessary "guests" that were living proof of their plans to commit election fraud, they had to clean up their act before word got out and ruined their peaceful image in the press!

A tremendous fleet of Greyhound, Continental Trailways and other buses amassed in Rajneeshpuram, and the entire population of guests were loaded onto these vehicles. They each were given amounts of cash and supplies of marijuana and shuttled away in the dark of night.

This enormous convoy of buses arrived on the streets of Portland starting around midnight, and their loads of transients were dumped all over the city. They hurriedly exited without protest at the behest of the armed security guards who kept everything orderly. The buses disappeared before the city police even knew this "dumping" had taken place.

Before the city of Portland even knew what had happened, their population had exploded with homeless people. Even if they could eventually prove a case against the city of Rajneeshpuram, Portland's budget would absolutely be drained, so the city officials had a mass meeting the next day to discuss the problem. Their solution to this situation was decided within hours. They did what any other "well run" American city would do; and they did so immediately!

Picture this: A massive fleet of buses, packed with street people; all fed and freshly showered, with clean clothing, each carrying an amount of cash and a bus ticket paid for; this tremendous fleet was soon heading south on Interstate Highway 5. With the aid of relief drivers, they timed their arrival to Los Angeles perfectly; the middle of darkness. Within a short time, the city of L.A. had a population increase of several thousand people.

One problem quickly solved; the Rajneeshees had one more idea to win the election; since they were fairly well accepted by the rural residents in Wasco County and a lot of local merchants were benefitting financially, there was still a chance of their winning the election, because a lot of their residents could show residency of six months or longer, so it could prove to be close. The Rajneeshees however could not afford "close;" they had too much at stake to risk it!

Now let's look at the next scene: The day before the Wasco County election, the city of The Dalles (county seat) was inundated with thousands of red-clad, smiling and laughing residents of Rajneeshpuram, and it was said to be a massive public relations effort and the news media reported it as such; a friendlier group of people could not be found.

The real reason for the show they put on was taking place in 10 restaurants in The Dalles. Behind the scenes, the Rajneeshees poisoned 10 salad bars with salmonella! No one died, but there were a tremendous number of very ill citizens of Wasco County who were prevented from being able to make it to the polls! Now the county had just cause for evicting the entire population of Rajneeshpuram as they quickly found out what had happened.

The authorities soon were swarming over what quickly would again become the "Big Muddy Ranch," because the population of Rajneeshpuram scattered like minnows in a trout pond! Millions of dollars went in so many directions, it was like driving down the road with a box of baby rabbits; every time you push one head down, another pops up, and everyone was going in different directions.

Krishnamurti Lake, Antelope, Oregon
Dedication stone along road to Rajneeshpuram reads: KRISHNAMURTI LAKE Reservoir Area 44 Acres Catchment Area 36 Square Miles Capacity 360,000,000 Gallons
By Tequask (Own work) [CC BY-SA 3.0 (https://creativecommons.org/licenses/by-sa/3.0)], via Wikimedia Commons

Authorities confiscated the Guru's 84 Rolls Royces, planes, properties, equipment and they tried to catch millions of dollars heading in 360 directions! However, the ones that got away did so in elaborate style.

If you are interested in learning more about the community of Rajneeshpuram, I recommend my friend Bert Webber's book, "Rajneeshpuram: Who Were Its People." It is out of print, but may be a few used copies available on Amazon.com.

7 CHASING BIGFOOT ON FOOT IS A NO-NO

Last summer my fiancé and I joined her brother and his wife for a camping trip on Lake Pend Oreille* in northern Idaho. They rented a cabin from some friends and invited us along.

We all live in Boise, so it meant driving from the bottom almost clear to the top of the state, but we were looking forward to totally relaxing for over a week and a half with nothing planned.

Aerial view of Lake Pend Oreille on the Pend Oreille River in 1993
By U.S. Army Corps of Engineers, photographer not specified or unknown [Public domain], via Wikimedia Commons

When we arrived in the town of Sandpoint, we spent the night in a motel, and while eating dinner in a café that night, a local resident came in and seated himself at the counter for a cup of coffee. So typical of a friendly, small town, a half dozen people greeted him, and the restaurant owner came out from the kitchen and casually (in his evidently normal loud voice) asked, "Any more on the Sasquatch yet?" The man responded with, "No, nothing much more, but the boy won't lose his arm." He went on to say the doctor had put two screws in it and it should be healed by the time school started in the fall.

The four of us were really curious as they were conversing on opposite stools, and now we could no longer hear; so finally, I couldn't stand it any longer, so I got up and wandered over to take a stool alongside the gentleman and introduced myself. I told them that our party was really interested in what happened, and I explained that we had just arrived in town on vacation and told them we were anxious to hear more.

They both began telling our group, as the others had gathered around, that a cabin near a place called Thompson's Outpost had recently been the scene of an unusual happening. After asking if we were familiar with the Bigfoot, we answered in the affirmative, explaining that Judy's (my fiancé) brother Tim had a friend who was an associate professor at Utah State and he had come up to Idaho for a seminar held by Dr. Jeff Meldrum; and these gentlemen immediately responded with enthusiasm. They both seemed very familiar with Dr. Meldrum, as he seemed to enjoy celebrity status in most of Idaho, as they said he was the absolute expert on Sasquatch!

They explained that a tourist's 11 year old son had seen what he described as a big, hairy orangutan, and since it took off running, he gained the courage to chase after it, and when it suddenly stopped by a large grove of pines, the kid threw a rock at it hitting it in the leg, and no sooner had it cried out in pain, a giant Sasquatch came from behind the tree, and with a loud roar, it came after the kid. He went running and screaming back to their cabin with the Sasquatch rapidly catching up.

The panicky brat was screaming at the top of his lungs, and just as it caught him by the arm and wrenched him to a stop, the kid's parents came around the corner and started yelling, more like the dad hollering and mom shrieking (according to other cabin residents), so the "Big Guy" dropped the kid and vanished! That's all they knew, but the café owner agreed to tell us more the next evening. We figured that to mean, "Buy dinner and I'll tell 'ya the rest of the story!"

The next morning as we left Sandpoint to make it to our rental cabin, we were all excited by the thought that we might encounter a Bigfoot, as our rental was close to the trading post, but in our entire time there, we never did see one. We did have more meals in that café however, and I think that we were in that 70 percent of visitors who, "Do not see Sasquatch."

P.S. ~ Boise, Idaho

*Publishers Note: Pend Oreille is pronounced **pond oh-ray**. The following information comes from the website boisestatepublicradio.org: The French name comes from fur trappers and it means "hangs from ears." That comes from the round shell earring worn by male and female Pend d'Oreille/Kalispel tribe members. To further the confusion, Idaho also has a town called Ponderay, and there's a Montana county called Pondera, all with the same pronunciation.*

8 NEW YEAR'S DAY SURPRISE

I was taking a friend home from a New Year's party. It was about
4:30 in the afternoon, and there were five of us in the car, including
my two children. We were traveling on a road I'd never been on
before on our way to Fowler, Michigan.

By RJ Feeny

I had my phone out getting ready to take a picture of some deer in
the field on the right hand side of the road. I happened to glance to
the left, and was like wow, what's that! I was driving about 55 mph,

so I just held the camera button down and took what pictures I could.

By RJ Feeny

Once I realized it sure looked like a Sasquatch, I slowed down and turned around, but he was gone. All five of us saw the creature; we couldn't believe our eyes!

RJ Feeny ~ Crystal, Michigan

9   SASQUATCH REFUGE IN A LAVA TUBE

A friend gave me your information, so finally after all these years, I can tell our story that we have told only among friends. My Bigfoot experiences happened back in the late 1960s, and at the particular time, I could not speak of it due to legal concerns. Then, like everything, it sat on the back burner till now.

Cave entrance stairway, Newberry Volcanic National Monument, OR
By MPSharwood (Own work) [CC BY-SA 4.0 (https://creativecommons.org/licenses/by-sa/4.0)], via Wikimedia Commons

It happened in the Newberry Cave system in central Oregon, where the government had suspended all caving and exploration for a period of time. There were two major reasons for their action suspending much of the visitation of Oregon's many caves. One was the belief that all bats were carrying rabies, so they had to cordon off all caves until their inspections could be done. The rabies theory later turned out to be false. In addition, the government had found that there had been human usage of the caves dating back to the 1300s, so the Federal Antiquities Act of 1906 was another of their reasons to block visitors from certain caves, hoping to find historic evidence that they did not want to disturb; which is understandable.

My particular adventure was with three friends, one of whom is my wife today. We had been anxious to explore some of the lava tubes in the system, as we had heard that many of them had networks over a mile long, so we stocked up on gear. When the day came, we arrived at our chosen cave, I don't recall for certain, but I believe it was named Wind Cave. We had our packs full of warm clothes in addition to the gear we were wearing, as these caves normally run around 35 to 50 degrees, we also had a supply of solid fuel heaters, flashlights (candles and carbide lights were prohibited), batteries, first aid kits, and we wore aluminum caving helmets; without which I would have no ears remaining! My wife remembers that I was continually banging my head as I walked too close to the sides, because it was harder packed sand and easier going.

Entrance to Lava River Cave, Newberry Volcanic National Monument, OR
By inkknife_2000 (7.5 million views +) [CC BY-SA 2.0
(https://creativecommons.org/licenses/by-sa/2.0)], via Wikimedia Commons

This tunnel system was part of the Newberry group, and I do remember vaguely that this particular volcano was connected to the Mount Mazama* System; around 7000 years old! We parked at the farthest end of the parking area, so anyone coming to this lot would maybe think we were day hiking through the trail system; just in case the "Mounties" came.

The cold air rushed to meet us and within a few minutes after entering the cave, so did the darkness. We were now in another world!

Lava River Cave, Newberry Volcanic National Monument, OR
By Dave Bunnell / Under Earth Images (Own work) [CC BY-SA 4.0
(https://creativecommons.org/licenses/by-sa/4.0)], via Wikimedia Commons

I had never before been in a cave except on a tour back in Dakota, but this cave was actually an empty lava tube! These tubes stretched out like rivers of molten lava, and as their surfaces cooled, they became like a tunnel, and as long as the volcano was erupting, and the upper surface was cooled by the air, it became a hollow passageway for the continual flow of lava that kept flowing and flowing. It's hard to tell from the surface that it's even under the rock, because the upper shell of lava spread out in all directions; from above it looks like solid rock, while underneath, the lava was still flowing inside this smooth-walled cave. When eruptions ceased, the remaining lava kept flowing out, and then it gradually cooled, leaving a tunnel. Over the centuries, sand from surface cracks and minor earthquakes covered the entire floor, so it mirrored the rounded tunnels over some of the highways and railroads of today.

Our party had plenty of batteries, and we each had small caver's lights attached to our helmets and flashlights in our hands. We weren't worried about bears being inside, as the entrance wouldn't allow anything that large past the gated opening, but we found small prints that may have been from fox and rodents. We did check for rattlesnakes, because we heard that the rattlers would hang around cave entrances to be able to move in and out depending on the air temperature as they lay waiting for prey; oh how carefully we checked!

We kept travelling down this tube, and to all of us, it felt like we were on a gradual descent, which may have been caused by imagination or because the erupting lava had been flowing down a hill, which actually disappeared when the lava flowed over it. That would be the logical reason, or the lava couldn't have kept going to empty the tube.

We were confronted with our first decision when after around 400 feet, the tube split into two tunnels; both roughly the same size. It appeared that the two floors each had about the same amount of traffic, as there were only divots where people or animals had trod, as no footprints were made in the soft sand. We decided to stay to our right on the way in, as it seemed slightly larger, and then "left when we left" to come out.

We next came to a very large opening where the ceiling of the tunnel had collapsed, leaving a huge pile of rock around 50 feet high, so we followed the obvious route where others had gone, and after about an hour of climbing up and down some pretty large (automobile-sized) rocks, we found ourselves back in our sand floored tunnel again. Here, while we had some rocks to use for tables and seats, we had lunch and took time to dump sand from our boots and relax awhile. We were conserving our lights on their lowest settings to extend their battery life.

Up ahead we heard a thumping, and I pictured a child running impetuously in front of its parents, so we all were watching the opening, fully expecting a family to momentarily emerge when one of our party sneezed from the ever present dust, and just at that moment, the footsteps stopped. We all thought it strange, but we reasoned that the child had heard the sneeze and retreated to the safety of its parents. Then the sound of footsteps started again, but faster and growing more distant.

Dismissing it as maybe our overactive imaginations, we packed up and continued on our way again, but I think we all caught ourselves casting our light beams further ahead and also on the cave floor. We thought it was quite strange that other "cavers" would not, out of common courtesy among explorers, have come to meet us, as it was obvious they knew we were there. We walked steadily for another hour without hearing anything other than our own footfalls; just treading in the same boring manner until suddenly, without warning, we emerged into a massive cavern.

This we had not expected, and due to the time of year, and the vague prohibition by the government on caving, we were without the customary brochures and printed guides they normally handed out. This cavern could easily have held a football stadium. Casting our light beams in all directions, we were doing our individual exploring when Trudy said, "Look up there," and she pointed to a portion of the ceiling on the far side of this dome, and then Tom said, "Lights off!"

His words needed no explanation as we went black. The blue sky was lighting up the far end of the cave. A huge section of this cavern had fallen in, and the gigantic rock mountain of rubble confronting us was made up of half the ceiling. As we sat silently on an immense flat section of rock and gathered our thoughts, something was making its way along the far wall, and it was not a person although it appeared to be walking on two legs. We had all seen it at the same time, and we all began whispering at the same moment!

The being seemed to walk almost like an orangutan, as it would dip its opposite shoulder and leg; as they seem to do when I'd seen them in zoos. The animal was carefully and soundlessly moving down the rubble pile until it was about on the cave floor and level to us. We momentarily lost sight of it, and no one even dared speak; not out of any fear, because it appeared much smaller than us, although we had no references to use for comparison at that distance.

I was glad that we had quietly entered this cavern, because the animal didn't appear to be moving in fear, but seemed perfectly at home. Finally after breathlessly standing there, the "monkey guy" reappeared at the far end of the opening where the lava tube was again in evidence, and it disappeared into the opening.

It seemed as if none of us had dared breathe, as we were all acting like we were out of breath as we began talking about what we had just seen. Hearts pounding with excitement, we determined this to have been a Sasquatch! We had all heard about the stories of "Ape Caves" across the Columbia River in Washington State, and that was not far from here, so we thought that may have been how those caves were named.

Entrance to Ape Cave from the interior ~ Gifford Pinchot National Forest
By Iwona Erskine-Kellie [CC BY 2.0 (http://creativecommons.org/licenses/by/2.0)], via Wikimedia Commons

We had been hearing about them being present throughout Oregon and the entire Northwest, but not being "outdoor type" people, we had never paid much attention. From what we had heard from friends who had actually encountered these Sasquatch, the Forestry department and all other government entities were in a total state of denial. They refused to even do more than accept a report; which it was said that the reports went directly into the trash according to confidential sources, and they had orders to keep all incidents under a cover of disclaimer. I was told by one of our friends that the government didn't want hundreds of Sasquatch hunters running around our huge forests shooting at everything that moves! They had done a confidential survey and the determination came back that they would need to double their budget if they admitted that Sasquatch was alive and well!

We were concerned, but this animal was obviously more afraid than we were, and since Jimmy and I were both carrying .38 revolvers, we felt safe enough to convince our friends to continue down the lava tube.

Lights back on again, we entered the continuance of the tube and we could plainly see the divots from the animal spaced as though it was running, so we put fears aside and about an hour later, we came to another open area, but this was different; it seemed like a giant dry pool of sand that opened up in the center, and there were two tunnels leading out from this point. Something may have caused the blockage and diverted the lava, but by this time we had come to a mutual decision that we would spend the night at this comfortable spot and continue deeper into the cave in the morning.

We had all but forgotten that the Sasquatch was somewhere in one of these tunnels, and we couldn't tell which of the passages it had gone into. The height of each tunnel was about seven or so feet, and they were both wide enough for two people to walk side by side, so we had chosen the right one in case there were more options up ahead.

Finally, we could relax completely, and we opted to use the left tunnel as our camp latrine, then we prepared the area we were now in for cooking and sleeping. This was quite an experience, as we had been in darkness all day, and even though it was early in the evening, after we ate, we were fairly well exhausted, so we climbed into our space blankets, with flashlights stuffed into our hiking shoes and guns in jacket pockets right by our heads; we slept soundly.

Soundly that is, until we were suddenly sitting up scrambling for lights and guns, because something else was in the cavern with us! As my light clicked on, I was confronted with a huge animal leaning over me, and I had smacked into its leg when I reached for my flashlight. The animal was as shocked as I was, and it let out a sort of screech, that in retrospect, reminded me of an alley cat's scream. Then, two more of the animals joined in the screaming as they ran by us and plunged into the blackness of the tunnel.

There, we parted ways, as they raced down the tunnel back towards the way we had come in. We all began scrambling to turn on more lights until we had the place looking like a newsroom. We had seen enough to know it was a Bigfoot family!

A noise suddenly emerged from where our guests had departed, and it sounded like one of them had fallen down; and then it occurred to us that they would have had no light at all. It became obvious that we must have driven them out of the large cavern where we first saw the smaller one, and they must have run before us up the last distance to where we ate. We surmised that they had used the light from our own lights to stay ahead of us, but when we camped, they must have been hiding in one of the other tubes in darkness except for the reflection from our beams.

Only after we had turned out our lights and fallen asleep did they dare to venture out, but being as there was no light to go by, one of them had stepped on my hand, and all hell broke loose, as they say! We were quickly packed up, and with extra lights on, we headed back up the cave toward the entrance. Not knowing if they could block us in by dislodging rocks, we were not anxious to find out. They hadn't seemed hostile, but fear is what makes most animals dangerous to humans, so we quickened our pace.

Periodically, we turned off our flashlights for a few moments to try to figure how these Sasquatch could navigate any of these tunnels; we soon had our answer. As the sun had begun to show signs of life, and even without our lights, we could easily navigate for a long ways down the tube. The sun coming through that huge hole in the cave's roof reflected throughout the tubes, likely due to what seemed like a sprinkling of gypsum or something sparkling in the walls of the tunnels.

We stopped for another rest at the monstrous cavern, and we carefully approached with lights out and slowly peered around the corner before entering, and way up just below the hole in the ceiling, we caught a glimpse of a brown shape exiting over the edge to the outside.

We finally reached the entrance and we were met with a swat team! Not actually, but there were two sheriff's vehicles with lights flashing and four officers about to enter the cave with hands on their guns. They seemed as surprised to see us as we were to run into them.

Even though it was early in the morning, a local resident had been walking his dog up toward the top of the flat topped hill above us, and he had reported what he said were several human screams that sounded like someone was being murdered! We all looked at each other, and then as if rehearsed ahead of time, we all laughed and responded with the story that we were taking turns scaring each other in the dark. Good thing we thought fast, as if we had told about the Sasquatch, we may have been in trouble for sneaking in the cave in the first place; although we may have become famous!

Apologizing for not realizing anyone was anywhere near this place, we packed up and got out of there with our best kept secret. What we will always have is the fact that Sasquatch is real!

Anonymous ~ Deschutes, Oregon

Publishers note: According to the U.S. Geological Survey, "Mount Mazama is one of the major volcanoes of the Cascades Arc. Crater Lake is located within the collapsed caldera of Mount Mazama on the crest of the Cascade Range in southern Oregon about 90 km (55 mi) north of the city of Klamath Falls and about 100 km (60 mi) northeast of Medford. This volcano formed at the intersection of the Cascade chain of volcanoes with the Klamath graben, a north-northwest low-lying basin that is surrounded by tectonic faults, and is bounded to the east by the Basin and Range province."

Crater Lake, Oregon
By werner22brigitte (Pixabay)

The entirety of Mount Mazama is located within Crater Lake National Park.

10 DON'T DYNAMITE SASQUATCH

I have been debating whether I dared to submit this story as it could possibly send me to jail, so for this reason I have not included my name. I just finally would like to have it in writing for my kids. I don't wish to be melodramatic, but you'll see why shortly.

More than a few years ago, when I was a teen, my family owned property on the Rogue River where we had a small (for family only) farm with a few animals and chickens.

A view of the Rogue River from Mount Reuben

An old, abandoned gold claim was on government land very nearby, and my father had found "color," so he could meet the requirements to file his claim. From production records from the past history of the mine, he had determined that the old mine could produce enough gold to make his one-man operation a very nice retirement income.

The mistake Dad made in his excitement was to mention his plans to a co-worker that he had worked alongside at the mill for the last 15 years; that was his undoing!

Entrance to the Pyx Mine

My dad went to the court house in Grants Pass, Oregon to file his claim, as he had already done the requirements of posting the claim with the old, but still used, method of putting notice in a glass jar, and he nailed the yellow claim notices on two nearby trees.

He said, as he went up the courthouse stairs to file, he was taking two of the large marble steps at a time. When he told the clerk of the location where he wanted to file, Dad said the clerk's forehead wrinkled slightly as he opening the filing cabinet, removed a file, and returned to the counter, and slightly shaking his head, he said, "I'm sorry sir, but that property was filed on three days ago."

When Dad saw the name of his now former friend, his heart just sank, and as he was returning to the car, he said he was shaking with a combination of anger and the extreme shock of having his dream shattered! As soon as he could, he phoned the traitor, but as our family listened, we saw that Dad was getting nowhere, even with an offer to pay the man to back away out of "fairness;" as it was my dad who told him about the claim.

Anyway, there was sadness in our home after that. At school the next week, I was telling a friend who also lived on the river about a mile upstream from us, and his retort gave me the idea to do what I did next.

My buddy had reacted with, "If that happened to my dad, I know he'd blow up that mine!" I knew that his family had a mine on their property and my mind was immediately made up; he agreed to sneak out a couple of sticks of dynamite as he often helped his dad set the fuses and was very familiar with the safe procedures. I reacted like a bass to a lure, and in two days my friend met me on the road and handed me a package. What the securely wrapped parcel held, were four sticks of dynamite and a long fuse. After giving me instructions on how to use it, we went back to our homes.

The following Sunday, I put on my backpack and headed out down along the Rogue River until I was opposite the area where the old mine was; I carefully crossed the road and followed the old overgrown road up to the place where a timeworn gate hung open. I stepped through it and climbed the steep trail to the mine entrance which was quite well hidden. It was the lower of two openings that Dad thought may have connected, but he hadn't ever been very far inside; just far enough to find evidence of gold, and he didn't want anyone to see him there, because that particular mine did not appear on any printed records.

I hurriedly placed my dynamite inside behind one of the support timbers that was braced by 8"x8" timbers on each side and covered it with several large chunks of rock. Lighting the fuse, I quickly ran out and down the hill toward the gate. I had barely jumped over the hanging gate when the dynamite exploded!

Even though it was inside the cliff wall and around a corner from the road, it made a huge explosion, and dirt flew out of the shaft like a cannon had shot it. The dust covered everything, and then I had my answer on whether the two tunnels met; as a huge cloud of dust, smoke and ash blasted out of both adits, and then, of all things, I was shocked and so sorry, as three large ape-like animals dashed out of the high opening and sprinted across the side of the slope and into the timber that covered the incline. One of the creatures was slightly limping.

Pyx Mine tunnel

I had heard stories about the "Sasquatch apes" ever since I was a kid, and the many part-Indian children of the mining families that had originally moved to the Rogue River from the Klamath Tribe whose fathers were white gold miners, had a lot of superstitions about these huge animals. They were common knowledge to the locals, and they even perpetuated and built up the stories to discourage visitors.

Looking back after all this time, I remember the Sasquatch to have been around six feet tall or larger, but it was hard to judge, except comparing their height to the mine adit entrance timbers. The largest one seemed about seven feet and the other two, maybe a foot or so shorter.

In retrospect, I wasn't able to tell anyone about these animals, because I could have gone to jail for a long time for what I had done, so I lived with my guilt all these years.

Anyway, as far as the mine; after life settled down to normal once more, and hostile threats toward the county recorder, from Dad's friends who were miners, had absolved my dad from any part in it, one plausible explanation was that lightning may have struck an old dynamite cache inside the mine entrance, and since no one could prove different, the subject was dropped, because all of our families had closely stuck together after the Indian Wars, so the incident was forgotten and my dad and the other man shook hands. Dad filed his claim, as the other man had no more interest in having to come several miles "to start over," and since Dad lived just yards from the location. I remember my dad saying the judge really wanted to "hang someone" for the incident, and he never did find out about the Sasquatch, but I made my family aware, and Dad did tell me that, "Your grandfather used to feed them." Dad had never before spoken of these animals, but he said every now and then a chicken would disappear, and they seemed to have a preference for cantaloupe and watermelons, but they avoided any human contact, so that's why he never mentioned them. Dad's new motto was, "The only way you can keep anything secret is to never tell a soul, including your dog!"

Dad said that many years ago, several of the creatures lived behind the mine area up higher in the forest, and he and Mom would leave potatoes and other vegetables out on a log behind the outbuilding, and they always took them. My older brother said that a new baby was born to their clan a couple of years ago, but several hunters had shot at it up on the old mine road, and he had thought the whole family of them left the area for good.

Our family knows about the Sasquatch, as do the rest of our extended community. Most of the residents from Marial, all the way down to Gold Beach have Native American blood, mainly from the Klamath Tribe, and the Sasquatch is well known among them. There is no question as to the validity among our mountain residents. It is part of our lives; a very lonely but interesting life.

Anonymous ~ Agness, Oregon

11 SASQUATCH; ON THE TRAIL OF HEROES

My wife and I were taking an extended vacation during the summer of 2002, and we spent over two months exploring some of the most beautiful national and state parks. While we were driving on the northwest side of Zion National Park in Utah, we were in the Kanarra Mountain area and we came upon a marble marker paying tribute to a World War I, most highly decorated hero named Captain Maurice F. "Maury" Graham.

Kanarra Canyon
The Dye Clan [CC BY-SA 3.0 (https://creativecommons.org/licenses/by-sa/3.0)], via Wikimedia Commons

On this remote scenic hilltop, we read that after the war, "Maury" Graham was flying the mail during a blizzard on January 10, 1930 against the advice of the Las Vegas airport and headed for Salt Lake City. It stated that Captain Graham knew that his cargo had some very important contents that needed to get there fast, so he left anyway in spite of the danger; his final act of devotion to a grateful nation!

The terrible snowstorm forced him down in the Kanarra Mountains, but Mr. Graham had landed successfully and was able to walk away from the landing, but he died several days later descending the mountain. He wasn't found until later the next year, but he was miles from the crash site, and no roads or people were anywhere near.

The monument said he was found because someone saw some kind of wheat-like plant growing behind a log, and they went to see what it was as it was all in one tall stalk; it was evidently from some seeds Mr. Graham had been chewing to help him quit smoking. The seeds had obviously sprouted, and upon being noticed, his body was recovered along with the mail, that even at the end of his life, he was still protecting!

We were both caught up in wondering what his terrible experience must have been like, so we gathered information from local area property owners and prepared to make the trek to where they found Mr. Graham as his memorial was only a few miles away from the actual site which was located on private land. The ranchers were so gracious in allowing us to even park on their property.

We were driving a mini motorhome, so we packed enough food and water in our knapsacks and with our GPS unit; we headed off in search of the poor man's last journey. We had some very good directions, so we took the shorter route up through their pastureland.

We tried to picture what it must have been like to make this hike while wounded and in deep snow through a terrible blizzard! Finally, thanks to a short, but flagged monument; we found the location deep in meadow grass, and then we went off to an area shaded by some mature trees and found a nice place for an overnight stay. We left our gear and went back to pay our respects to a hero's memory.

As we sat on a deteriorating log contemplating what the poor man must have felt like when he finally reached this location, Toni suddenly turned and shouted out, "Get away!" I immediately saw what had drawn her attention; some large, shaggy brown ape-like critter was running down the hill with one of our packs. Now I was hollering at it as well, and I lobbed a rock in its direction, and it must have hit close, because it dropped the pack and plunged into a steep gulley, and when we caught up to the spot, we heard sounds from further down the slope, as the animal must have still been headed downhill.

We went back to our campsite and noticed the animal's large footprints in the clay soil on a bare spot; the imprint of one of the feet dwarfed my size eleven boot. It seemed to be maybe seven feet tall, or even more, and although we were just guessing, it weighed maybe 200 pounds and was thin-looking for its height. It must have seen us sitting there as it stole the pack; which was very unusual for wild animals, or maybe it just happened on it and hadn't noticed us until we yelled, because then it really took off fast!

We made a cold camp that night; we kept a fluorescent lantern hanging in the tree above us, and neither of us felt like we dared sleep. It was around 12:30 or 1:00 in the morning when we were suddenly bombarded with flying pieces of hard clay, dirt balls and rocks! We sought shelter on the uphill side of two large pines, and I dug into my pack for my small pistol, and aiming at the dirt by a tree, I fired two shots; I didn't want to hurt these animals; after all we were the ones trespassing in their home. That stopped everything but our hearts, which were still beating loudly!

We spent the few hours until dawn huddled against the morning chill, trying to feed the small fire we had built, as we did not dare to lie down. As the dawn chased the remaining shadows from our edge of the forest, we heard a rapping sound, such as made by smacking a hard object against a hollow stump; kind of a "thunk." This sound was repeated in three short, but loud thumps, and immediately afterward, these same sounds were echoed from further into the forest, and then we heard answering sounds from at least two more places. Leaving our lantern faintly glowing behind us, we quietly sneaked away; we felt it safe to leave, because it was battery operated, so we sacrificed it to distract the animals from our escape!

Arriving back at our vehicle, we quickly made our way to see the nice property owners who had been so helpful, and as we were comfortably seated on their sprawling patio, we told our story in spurts; each of us remembering different details.   Then with refreshments served, we gained our composure enough to calmly listen as these nice people confessed that they had "certainly hoped" that we wouldn't run into their Sasquatch neighbors, but they thought it best to keep their secret, because privacy is why they lived so far from people in the first place, and they were sure the animals of this area must have the same feelings.

We had both heard many stories about the Sasquatch and Bigfoot, but never before had we heard of any sightings of them in southern Utah! These people said they have protected their discovery for almost five years now since several colonies of them had moved in, and they have lived with the occasional loss of a calf or sheep now and then, but these Sasquatch mostly hunted wild game, and the rancher's assumed that they had come here from Colorado where there reportedly were many of them, because it was not all that far away; just over a few short mountains which we could see in the distance.

Before leaving, we thanked them for their courtesy, and as promised, we will give no further details at to our actual directions, but the experience we had was absolutely true!

Jack and Toni Crosby ~ Rapid City, South Dakota

12 SASQUATCH VS DAVY CROCKETT

My great grandfather, Tobias Rahlstrom, had an interest in a gold claim on the Rogue River back sometime in the early 1900s, and I remember as a boy being absolutely enthralled with him the only time I ever saw the man. I was about 10 years old when this bearded, grizzled and bent over man stayed at my parents' house for a couple of weeks. I don't have too clear a recollection of why he stayed so long, but I remember when he arrived in our small home in the city of Rogue River, Oregon. What fascinated me most about this man was the fact that he was a "real gold miner!"

Flume ditch used to channel water for mining operations

My grandfather had worked at a mill until he was killed when a load of logs rolled off the rail car and crushed him, so I never really knew my grandfather, but here was my living, breathing great grandfather who to my young mind must surely be the "spittin' image" of Davy

Crockett! His leather shirt and pants fit my conjured up image perfectly.

Whisky Creek Cabin on the Rogue River ~ built about 1880 by an unknown gold prospector

Night after night, this spellbinding storyteller would keep us mesmerized in front of the fireplace as he told of his adventures along the Rogue River; and especially of the "skunk ape" (now known as Sasquatch) when it tore apart his cabin on the Rogue! I sat silently by as youngsters did in those days, enthralled by such excitement.

Great granddad talked about having built what sounded like a very crude log and mud structure down the river from a casual acquaintance of my father's, named Cy Whitneck, who traded Dad gold for mining tools that Dad made in his off-time during winters when they couldn't log due to the terrible conditions. We had some mention of Mr. Whitneck in some paper when Rogue River City was still Woodville.

Granddad said that none of the miners were very close to each other's claims in those days, because they all fiercely guarded their claims from thieves. I remember Granddad telling us this after all these years, because I gave a report to my schoolmates on the topic, on which Mr. Lenmark gave me an A. The reason I remember it so well is I must have drove my mom nuts as I recited it maybe a hundred times to practice.

Anyway, it seems that Granddad caught two strangers on his claim and they exchanged words; the men refused to leave, and one of the men fired a rifle at Grandfather, and he ran as fast as he could upriver to Mr. Whitnecks' claim. They picked up another miner and the three of them, with their guns, hurried down the well-traveled pathway above the river.

As they neared the area where Grandfather's claim was, they heard several shots and ducked down quickly, realizing that the gunshots were not far from them. Then they heard a loud scream, then another gunshot, and a very loud screech and another scream. Going faster now, Grandfather said they came upon one of the men lying across the trail; his arm had been torn almost off, and he said the bones were sticking out and there was blood all over the leaves and the ground. (No wonder when I was reciting this to my class, my teacher turned pale and sat down!) The man had no pulse. Then he said they heard another scream further downriver, and they ran down the path.

I remember in my excitement of hearing the story, interrupting by asking, "What's a skunk ape?" Granddad said to be patient, as he was getting to that part, and he continued. He said, around the next curve there was a big, hairy, apelike animal. It looked kind of like a shaggy ape, but it seemed to be much thinner and about seven feet or so tall. He said this animal is seldom a bother unless it's hungry or if you interfere with its young. It's highly protective from having encountered men before; they seem to urinate when they are frightened, and oftentimes all over themselves and it smells horrible. The local Indians call it Sasquatch!

Anyhow, the animal just leaped to the side and in two seconds it had disappeared into the underbrush. Searching the area, they found blood at the rocky shore downriver, but no sign was ever found of the other claim jumper.

The records show a "fall" as the cause of death for the man they did find, as in those days, nobody had time for inconveniences, because as Granddad explained, it was too hard to find enough gold in that rocky place to waste time with things that were done with, and especially since the men were crooks after all, no one wanted to lose any more time on them.

At my age then; this was the most excitement I had ever had, and I made lots of notes. For a few weeks, I was the most popular kid in the school.

Granddad had never really explained more about the skunk ape, because he said it was most often called a Sasquatch, or as a group of miners down by Marial town called it "Hairy;" and even though you'd think these men and their Indian wives would have communicated more, times were hard, so socializing was not as common as one would think.

Tyee Rapids, downriver from the Whisky Creek Cabin

I've carried the memory of this experience all of my life and now if it makes your book my great grandfather's story will live on.

Andy Rahlstrom ~ Oregon

13 SASQUATCH OF THE CALIFORNIA COAST

Our experience actually happened two years ago in January. We were reluctant to discuss it beyond our close friends in our housing area, as we are new to Northern California. While Crescent City people seem to be familiar with the Sasquatch, our friends in Southern California would think we were nuts! Our new friends finally convinced us to submit our story, and if you publish it, we can all have copies on our coffee tables. Since this happened, all our neighbors have binoculars and hike more often.

As we often do in the winter; in January 2016, we were at the parking area south of Crescent City in a part of the Redwood National Park, which is on the ocean side almost across from the Del Norte Coast Redwoods State Park.

Redwood National Park (Pixabay)

We were sitting in the car facing the Pacific Ocean, and the occasional spray would hit the rocks just right and come crashing over our roof; and out of the corner of my eye on the driver's side window I saw a shadow, that when I turned, looked like a young child in a parka. I turned to my wife Pat and told her to look. As she looked out my side window, another much larger figure ran down the sand dune outside the parking lot after the smaller one.

We thought it strange that these people would be out past the parking lot and down near the heavily crashing surf when we were the only car in the entire lot. There also were no vehicles across the highway, so Pat remarked that they must have come all the way from somewhere in the Redwood Forest where there were campsites.

The wind was blowing the rain and surf so hard; we couldn't see much other than the shadows out beyond a hundred yards. All of a sudden, the larger shadow came up and over the dune directly in front of our car and it was carrying the smaller one; in seconds it was right before us and we got the shock of our lives! It wasn't a person at all. It looked like some kind of a huge, long-haired gorilla, and its thick fur was drenched with water. It hadn't looked like a gorilla, except for its shaggy, long hair, but its jawline was more wolf like!

It hadn't seen us, and when it finally did it was almost right at our hood. That's when I turned on the headlights, and you'd have thought it had been shot. It stopped dead! Then, it was almost like it didn't know what we were and it tilted its head to the left and right, as though straining to see. We figured afterward that it was just trying to see if our car was occupied. It was then that Pat let out a startled scream, and the poor critter looked at her, then back at me, and turned back toward the ocean and absolutely flew around the distant dune! It must have been covering 10 feet with each leap.

Now I recovered from my temporary paralysis of senses and I jumped out of the car without even closing the door, and I ran behind and to the left of that sand hill and toward the highway. My thoughts were that this animal wouldn't go into the ocean, and it must have to turn toward the forests across the highway. I had no sooner finished the thought when there it went; crossing the entire highway and both ditches in what couldn't have been over three giant strides, and then it sped across a large area of tall grasses, maybe like a swamp. I was still standing by the highway when it entered the dark forest about three hundred feet away. In retrospect, I wondered what I would have done if I had caught up with it; scream?

I came out of my trance when a passing trucker blew his horn as he presented me with about 10 gallons of water from his trailer tires. I slogged back to the car, and Pat and I sat there discussing what we had experienced while I had the heat on high and we endured the steam from my soaked clothing.

Battery Point Light ~ Crescent City, California
By Reiseblogger (Pixabay)

After talking with two selected couples in our neighborhood, who we felt wouldn't think we were crazy, we found out that they had also seen these Sasquatch, as they called them, although they said they'd never been as close to them as we were.

After that, we kind of kept the experience to ourselves until one couple loaned us your book, "They Saw Sasquatch," that had a story in it from an acquaintance of theirs in Oregon. So here is our submission and we look forward to maybe seeing more of these neighbors in fur coats!

Pat and Ralph Dempsey ~ Crescent City, California

14 KILLER DOGS SCARED STRAIGHT

I am originally from Oregon, and I was back there a few years ago when I had an experience that was so frightening that I told only a very few people. This happened back in 2009, and I always wished more people could know about it, until my Uncle Ed Fogerty told me about your Swan Literary website. I look forward to getting my story in a book for all of my friends and family to see.

I live now in Borger, Texas up by Amarillo and our Lake Meredith is almost a twin to Oregon's Lake Billy Chinook over near Madras. Your Metolius River runs through that lake like the Canadian River flows through Texas' Lake Meredith.

To continue, back in 2009, my wife and I were up visiting family in Oregon. Uncle Ed and I had spent time camping and fishing at Lake Meredith a couple of years back when he came to Texas, and he made a comment about how the two lakes were so much alike they could be twins; so then and there we got things together and the two of us packed our supplies and Eddy's aluminum boat, and three days later we were camped in the Cove Palisades State Park in Oregon.

The country was beautiful and they were having a hot spell, but at least it was the dry heat of the desert country that I prefer. The ranger came by our camp and apologized, but said he was posting the lake against fishing for two days due to some fingerlings they were dumping into the lake from the Warm Springs Indian Reservation side and they wanted to make sure they disbursed properly before allowing us to disturb the waters. We were in no hurry and we pretty much had the campground to ourselves, as it seemed like everybody else must have known about this fish stocking but us.

There was one other pickup with a large camper on the back and the people had two young, but huge dogs. They were some sort of Bull Mastiffs or whatever, but as we were walking near their campsite they were straining at their chains making the god awfulest growling and slobbering I'd ever seen. The owners seemed like nice folks and they came away from their camp to say hello; they explained that they were breeders and this outing was to socialize the dogs before their new owners came to pick them up, as they needed to get used to people. Judging from the ferocity of those monsters, we figured it would take a lot more socializing, only not with us!

Lake Billy Chinook
Public Domain, https://commons.wikimedia.org/w/index.php?curid=512160

Our first full day was spent by hiking along the northern corner of the lake, and around the corner across the Metolius River was all the Indian Reservation. We saw the other campers hiking up by the large bend where the river entered the lake and those large dogs looked almost like bears the way they lumbered through the meadow. Across the river was *Mount Jefferson* and *Three Fingered Jack*, and I hadn't seen these majestic mountains for so many years that I was standing there and taking in all of the beauty when suddenly, I heard loud, fierce barking and saw the explosive charge of those monstrous dogs as they charged through a distant field.

Their owners were standing there blowing frantically on their shrill whistles and the dogs were running all out, with their leashes trailing in midair, and they quickly disappeared into a patch of dense pine trees surrounded by berry bushes.

Three Fingered Jack, a heavily eroded volcano in the Cascade Range in Oregon
By Ericshawwhite (Own work) [CC BY-SA 3.0 (https://creativecommons.org/licenses/by-sa/3.0)], via Wikimedia Commons

We could only stand there and listen to the loud barking, and then there were deeper sounds like snarling, and then a horrible scream like something had been really hurt bad, and after that, not a sound except the wind.

Eddy and I were up further on the hillside when two figures burst from the trees headed up the back of the ridge, but they weren't the dogs. They were large apelike animals, but they ran on two legs, and if it hadn't been for the coats of long hair standing out in the wind, neither of us would have paid them any mind, but we could see they weren't human!

Then down the slope, we saw the two dogs running downhill and they were both limping, one especially bad, and barely able to drag his back legs. The other one had only a slight limp, but even from our distance away, we could see that it was bleeding at the shoulder and neck.

Meanwhile, we had both swung our gazes back to the "boogie men" and now in just a matter of a minute; they had gained the thick forest that enveloped the rest of the mountainous canyon ridge.

Then all was quiet, but for the faint whining and the occasional yip from the poor dogs. We went over to see if we could help the people, and by the time we got there, they had managed to pressure stop the one's bleeding and put medication from their backpack's first aid kit on the wounds; enough to evidently ease the poor animal's pain somewhat. There didn't seem to be any broken bones, but the more severe cuts and places where the fur had been torn or sliced off were obviously painful, and both dogs kept licking at their semi-bandaged wounds.

We accompanied the folks back to their camp, which took an hour or more due to allowing for the slowly limping dogs. They were far too large and heavy to carry. Discussing what had happened as we returned to camp, we discovered that these people had not seen the animals that the game warden later identified by our description as Sasquatch! There had evidently been pine trees between themselves and the dogs enough so as to completely block their view.

When Eddy and I told them what we had witnessed, they were absolutely astounded! They asked us several times to repeat our descriptions of the Bigfoot animals, because they said they had many friends who claimed to have had sightings and encounters with these animals, but here they were, having their dogs in a fight with them and missing the whole thing!

You know, there is only one thing that was even less understandable and totally disappointing; the unimaginable and ridiculous fact that this whole time I had a camera in my fatigue vest's front pocket and I didn't even think about it until I took my vest off back at camp. When I mentioned it to Ed, he said my secret was safe with him, and he hadn't thought about it either. By the time the dogs and their people left, the dogs seemed to be okay, but they certainly acted very docile and tame. I guess you could say they were now socialized!

Mountain Man ~ Borger, Texas

15 LIVING AMONG SASQUATCH AND THE HIPPIES

Back in 1969 my boyfriend and I and a few friends from California moved to the Southwest corner of Oregon to join more friends who had gone before us to join a free life minister*. We were invited to become members of their group, which at the time, were commonly called hippies. We joined them outside of Cave Junction, Oregon where the surroundings were absolutely out of this world!

The historic Store Gulch Guard Station No. 1020 (built 1933), located on Illinois Valley Road By Ian Poellet (Own work) [CC BY-SA 3.0 (https://creativecommons.org/licenses/by-sa/3.0)], via Wikimedia Commons

Many of our people had moved into old abandoned shacks and log cabins scattered throughout the forests north of the Oregon Caves National Monument. Many of these ancient structures from Oregon's wild, gold mining days had been fixed up to be quite comfortable, and now that Oregon recently legalized marijuana, I guess I can dare to mention that back then when it was illegal, we made a nice living raising crops that left our community for places across the U.S.A. It has been said that this part of Oregon has the perfect pot growing climate, and it turned out to be true!

When we first arrived, we were placed in a fairly large cabin with two other couples, and we were detailed to work in one of the hidden grow operations. This particular patch was about 400 yards from a paved road that was seldom used anymore; since our group was occupying most all of this valley, and there were only a couple of property owners bordering on this state forest, we were pretty much ignored.

Our duties were not strenuous, but we were kept busy maintaining our water supply to make sure the crops turned out perfect.

Illinois River near Cave Junction, Oregon

Two days after we were introduced to our duties, we were arriving at our job when we were confronted by a large, shaggy ape-man who had stepped out on the trail ahead of us. It didn't appear all that surprised, as it just looked at us and then looked back in the direction it was headed, and continued through the forest of four to 12 foot trees. We were left standing there utterly in shock, but when we recovered enough to get back to camp, the others just said they had forgotten to warn us about the creatures they called Sasquatch!

We later found out that a lightning caused fire had torn through this area about 14 years before and accounted for hundreds of acres of damage, and this was the reason for the short trees.

The new growth was around 10 to 15 or so feet high, which combined with the large trees toppled by the fire, made a veritable maze. There would be a growth of 15 or more trees in a close clump interspersed with dead, crisscrossed trees up to 70 or so feet long. What logging roads that once ran through these forests were no longer useable.

That's what made this area perfect for not only growing the marijuana crops all over the entire long and vast valley, but what also made the authorities look the other way. That, and certain "peace offerings," allowed us to thrive with hardly any hassle from the authorities. Very seldom were we harassed by the law, except when the pressures from politicians moved them to occasionally bust one of our camps, but even then, there was only the occasional hand-slap and small fine, which we paid promptly through our group lawyer; just enough to go through the motions to keep the Feds from getting involved.

The Sasquatch didn't have any use for us, as I'm sure they were here first, but we more or less tolerated each other. Then one day, two of our people were hitchhiking back from the town of Grants Pass, when suddenly several rocks and large sticks came flying out of the trees and broke the guy's nose and left a large gash on his girlfriend's leg. They began to run along the shoulder of the highway hoping they could flag down a car headed for Cave Junction, but it was a very slow traffic day, so they were forced to run a great distance while continually ducking to avoid a missile now and then. Then they passed by a grassy area where the Sasquatch couldn't continue without being fully exposed to traffic and the attack stopped.

A lot of our activities were held as a group where we would gather in one particular depression where the tall trees soared to the heavens, and with trees about ninety and more feet high, we sat beneath two opposing ridges. This put our group so far below that even the infrequent aircraft surveillance planes couldn't see us. We had a good supply of dry firewood kept under lean-tos covered by tarps. No sign of smoke would betray our possessions and we knew from our many informants (customers) that there was very little reason for anyone to try to roust us from our peaceful surroundings.

One day however, one group of customers had come to transact some rather large buys at one of our harvestings, and they had been smoking pot and drinking alcohol when one of the younger Sasquatch came along, and the fools started shooting at it, and one of the shots hit it in the leg. The poor animal screamed and wailed terribly loud!

Siskiyou Mountains near the California – Oregon border

After that incident, we began having problems with the big animals. They would go through our grow areas in the night and tear up our water lines and uproot our plants, and we began taking turns standing guard over everything on a rotating schedule, and the necessity to stay on guard never let up, but tensions did ease a little when we would no longer allow our buyers to camp anywhere near our operations; we began transporting our harvests further south near the California – Oregon border north of Happy Camp, California. A lot of our shipments were taken barely into California, so if anyone got apprehended, it wouldn't involve Oregon law enforcement at all, and since the California border was in such a highly forested and mountainous location, the state of California wouldn't deem it important enough nor cost effective to station any number of officers there more than sporadically. Besides that, there were enough of their own citizens growing up there that they pretty much ignored us all.

Rough and Ready Botanical Wayside in Cave Junction, Oregon

Then, we also began to bring food offerings, like watermelon, cantaloupe, apples and peaches to our hairy neighbors, and soon, we could work peaceably once more.

We never got friendly enough with the very large Bigfoot (we assumed them to be males), but our relationship became a matter of tolerance once again.

After about two years, the adventure finally became annoying to me; living like tame animals, dressing in gypsy type clothing, and being shunned by the general populace. So I split with my boyfriend, took the fair amount of cash I had squirreled away, and returned to San Francisco. Two years later found me returning to the wonderful Southern Oregon climate where I found employment with a large real estate firm who never had any idea that I had lived in the forests only 30 miles away from my new home of Medford!

D.S. ~ Medford, Oregon

Publishers note: The lady that submitted this encounter included the name of the minister, but to protect his identity we have removed his name from the story.

16 PARTYING WITH BIGFOOT

I did not intend to invite Bigfoot to my birthday celebration, but here I was on my 21st birthday after finally being old enough to buy booze! This was several years ago when I lived in Two Harbors, Minnesota. My buddy and I stopped at a liquor store; I went in alone, sauntered up to the counter, and since I was in a lower wage scale, I ordered a bottle of inexpensive bourbon. I fully expected the man to ask for my ID since I looked so young and I purposely tried to look even younger on this particular day. To my absolute amazement and huge disappointment, he took my cash, packaged my bottle, gave me my change and told me to, "Have a nice day." Now, how could I have a nice day after waiting years for this opportunity, and he never even asked, even though I tried to act suspicious; what a waste!

As I got back in the car my friend Ernie asked me what was wrong, thinking the store clerk gave me a bad time. I didn't say anything and just pulled in to the store parking lot next door. We went inside for 7Up, ice, chips, dip and some other goodies and headed for Silver Bay; it was no big deal, just a ways north and we had our camping gear along.

There was a really pretty lake there that had just a very few picnic tables, no boat launching area, and as I hoped, there wasn't a soul around; not even tire tracks in the parking area. It was perfect, as I wanted to relax, legally drink, and take time to savor in my adult status.

As most of the guys in my age group did, we soon got tipsy; okay, drunk. I was glad after a couple of hours of trying to out drink each other, Ernie, who had done this same ritual three months before and knew what was coming, assured me that I would not spin into outer space! We left our drinks on the picnic table and he walked me down to the lake where I proceeded to fall on my knees in the cold but shallow water.

Splashing water on my face began to help me feel better until I lost my balance and nose-dived into a patch of waterlilies. Anyway, after about a half hour, we staggered (only slightly) back to resume our partying, but as we rounded the large bushes back at the picnic area, there was an extremely large ape-like animal standing near our picnic table.

He was drinking our bourbon and eating our food! He seemed oblivious to our presence, and we stood dumbfounded as this monster just tipped up the 7Up bottle and took a drink as a human would. Then it grabbed a handful of chips and the bottle of whisky. It shoved chips into its mouth and then took a drink of booze! It immediately spit it out in a spray that showed its disgust and plainly emphasized that it was smarter I!

I had often heard tales told by those who had seen the Sasquatch, so I was not totally scared to death, but between Ernie and myself, I think we were too drunk to run away and too frightened to speak. Had I not lived where these animals were fairly common, I might have broken my neck trying to get away. I was shaking so badly that I feared my neck would break anyway!

All of a sudden, the huge seven foot animal spun around and saw us, and he made a move to round the table and come toward us when he started to stagger. He grabbed a tree to steady himself and with a very loud, gurgly shriek, he threw up in a wide gusher! Then in bewilderment, he feel to his knees and shrieked again in a sort of high pitched yelp. He then staggered to his feet and ran straight away toward the lake, and here we were, ourselves hardly able to walk, stumbling after him.

As he hit the spot where we had just come from, he stopped and bent over and heaved again, and turned to run and fell into the lake. It made some sort of a yell, and switching from two feet to all fours, and then back again, he made it into the dark pine forest.

Ernie and I sat down and, as drunks will do, we slobbered all over ourselves trying to recall every detail of our encounter. We have shared our story, but we soon learned to lead into it carefully, because many people will listen intently and seem like they are really interested until they simply say, "You're nuts!" and walk away.

So, thought I'd share my 21st birthday encounter with you as it's been long enough ago, and I've heard of a lot of sightings of the Bigoot, so I feel that I can share it to be among others (not the drunks) who have also met Sasquatch!

Jimmy Westholm (the adult) ~ Sister Bay, Wisconsin

17 TIPTOE THROUGH THE TULES WITH BIGFOOT

My brother Jerry and I had a Bigfoot experience way back in 1952. We lived in Alturas, California, and a good friend and schoolmate invited us on a vacation neither of us will ever forget! We were offered a fantastic summer vacation; our friend Jim's father had a property up by Lower Klamath Lake that had been in their family since pioneer days.

Lower Klamath Lake, Siskiyou County, California
By Blake, Tupper Ansel (Fish & Wildlife Service) [Public domain], via Wikimedia Commons

Jim said their pioneer ancestors had been bound for the California gold fields, but their covered wagon had broken a wheel and it happened in such a beautiful place, his great great grandmother said she would go no further; so along with two other families from their party, they settled there and spent the rest of their lives farming the rich soil. The property was still in the family and when we got there, we could tell it had long since fallen into disuse and the only remaining sign of human habitation was an old log cabin on a low hill right in the middle of a ring of gnarly apple trees.

Here was our dream adventure and we were going to rough it. Jim's dad took the three of us up there in his '49 Dodge full of supplies and we were set to stay for a full month. We had all the food supplies one could imagine and our plans were to use the old woodstove in the cabin for cooking, boiling lake water for drinking and bathing, and since their family often had done this over the years, we felt safe. This was every boy's "dream" summer vacation!

There was an old, dead apple tree that was used as a ready source of wood for the stove and a cozy stone fireplace at one end. There were only two small four-paned windows in the kitchen and eating area, and another to the left of the fireplace. The roof had been maintained over the years, but as for the inside and outside logs, they looked tired and smelled moldy.

Jim's dad helped us unload our supplies, and off he went, with us slowly realizing that we were "off the grid" as we say nowadays. It would seem strange today to think of surviving without refrigeration, but as many kids our age did in those days, we all drank coffee, not that we liked it so much, but we didn't have a choice out where we were. We did have some soda with us, quite a lot really, which we planned to leave in the lake to keep it cool.

One of the first things Jim did was unpack three fishing rods, and taking a small tin can and an old rusty spade from the woodshed attached to the cabin, he proceeded to dig up the ground for worms. We all pitched in and soon we had a fairly decent bunch of these sacrificial wigglers, and off we went on a faint animal trail down the hill to the lake.

The forest grew thicker after we left the small orchard, and we could see the pretty, dark blue lake. There were no signs of other buildings, smoke, or anything to indicate neighbors. As we drew closer to the lake, the smells of vegetation were quite fragrant and fish were apparently feeding on the abundance of water bugs and flying insects as there were splashes everywhere.

Before we baited our hooks, Jim took off his shoes and we followed suite; he led us around a pathway in the bulrushes to a large screened-in box that sat in water about three feet deep. This was our first introduction to a fish trap. I guess you could look at it as a fresh fish storage tank. Jim explained that since fish were fairly moody feeders that there would be times where they would bite like crazy and times where they didn't, so the idea was to catch extra fish when they were biting and save some for when they weren't. Jim further explained that the wide mesh of the screen allowed minnows to swim in and out as they fed on small critters in the sandy bottom, and the bigger fish in the trap could eat, until they in turn, could be eaten by us; quite resourceful!

We happened to make quite a haul with the three of us standing in the rushes and flipping our bait into the dark, deep water and soon we had enough for three meals, so we took enough for eating and put the rest in the trap. Back at the cabin, we had a really enjoyable meal, and realized how the original settlers had to do this every day, as all meat could quickly spoil.

Between swimming, hiking and adventuring through the heavily forested hills surrounding the lake, we were having a great time until one day when Jerry returned from his trip to fetch dinner from our fish trap with no fish! We were all certain that we had about four of them from the day before, so off we went to inspect our screens, but nothing appeared to be amiss, so we dug some worms and returned to refill our larder.

We puzzled over the situation and just assumed that maybe one of the long-beaked terns or other bird had somehow managed to open the hinged lid, but obviously sound reasoning was not a part of it. We were lucky in catching fish over the next hour as we spread out along the shore, and taking three fish for dinner, we put three more in the cage. This time I wrapped the small hasp on the lid with the loose wire that we had not been using, and realized precisely why it was hooked there.

The next morning, we went for a hike along the trail that meandered on the hillside along the lake, and as we were wading a shallow creek bed that fed into the lake, there in the three inch deep water were two huge footprints! They were maybe more apparent, because we were looking carefully in the clear water for agates. We became more unnerved when there in the damp sand just before the grass, was an absolutely clear print that was beginning to slowly fill with water as we watched.

At first we thought it was human, but for as clear as it was, there was no ball at the toes' end and the ball of the foot where the toes start wasn't there; the toes did show evidence of long, sharp claws though!

Even with the question of "claws" unanswered; all three of us immediately bounced to a standing position and began circling around in search of this person with these monstrously big feet. The area was heavily overgrown with willows and wiry brush that we weren't able to see over, but with these prints being what must have been over size 12 or 13, we reconsidered our bravado and rather hurriedly made our way back to higher ground, and Jim climbed up an old elm tree to search the area.

Jim was balancing on two separate limbs of the tree when he let out a gasp and yelled as he pointed; "There's some kind of bear running on its hind legs!" By the time Jerry and I made it up another tree, there was nothing to be seen.

We quickly retreated to the cabin where we nervously sat outside watching in different directions until we returned to normal by carefully reasoning that if it meant us harm, the animal was certainly big enough to overpower all of us at once. Since it didn't, we calmed down and went fishing, as we couldn't live on hardtack biscuits and canned beans and fruit with any degree of enjoyment.

Now that we had determined what was stealing our fish, we caught six, and now had eight fairly decent crappies and bass. This time we tied the trap shut with a length of heavier wire and returned to the cabin. We were still stewing over the animal Jim had seen, because we all knew that bear do not run on two legs, and even though we had heard a lot about Sasquatch, we thought they were only in the mountains.

It had now turned dark as we finished cooking our daily fish dinner when we heard an awful scream. The sound was shrill and started with a kind of wail like something was hurt and scared, and then it ended with a much louder and longer combination of howl and furious growling. These various sounds continued for several minutes, and then suddenly, something smashed into the cabin wall!

We made sure the door was locked and we propped some firewood against it at an angle, and there we stood; Jim had the axe, Jerry held a shovel, and I was poised to strike with a piece of pipe that normally functioned as a clothes hanging rod.

I found myself trembling, but it must have given up, and I'm sure the others were also relieved, but our fears were never discussed afterwards. The rest of the night passed with no further sounds.

At the first light of dawn, we were up with weapons in hand, and slowly we dared venture into the yard, carefully searching around the cabin with the door left open for a hasty retreat. We found a piece of log and a large stone near the cabin door, but nothing more. Our courage had returned in daylight, so we walked down to the fish trap, and we could see from a distance what we surmised to be the source of the first anguished scream from the night before.

Our fish trap was totally destroyed; it had been ripped apart with screen and wood strewn all over the shore. We all saw what appeared to be a large amount of blood on some of the dry wood, and it also looked like blood splattered on some of the rushes. Whatever happened, the animal must have been badly hurt, and we felt bad about that. We stayed around the cabin the rest of the day, and we ate from cans that night.

The next morning we heard the most welcome sounds of all, Jim's dad was driving down the road to check on us, and how welcome he was! After he patiently listened to our individual interpretations of our encounters, he knowingly nodded his head, saying something like, "I haven't heard of the Sasquatch being seen in years, but from your descriptions, it appears to have returned." He then reiterated several stories from his youth when family members told of their past meetings with several of these animals, and it seems that they had once been more numerous before there were so many automobiles. Then he surprised us all in saying, "Hope the poor guy is okay!"

Ronald K. ~ Boise, Idaho

Publishers note: The title of this chapter comes from the freshwater marsh plant "Tule" which thrives in Lower Klamath Lake as well as most fresh bodies of marsh in North America.

18 ANOTHER SECRET AT LAKE X

It was back in the early 60s that a friend of my father introduced me to Mr. Elmer Carl Kiekhaefer, the owner of Kiekhaefer Corporation and Mercury Marine. At the time, it was the hottest company in the entire U.S.A.

I had grown up in a boating family, so I was genuinely impressed to meet him; talk about timing! After the introductions were made, Mr. Kiekhaefer told me he liked my handshake and we spoke for a while about how much I knew about boats and motors; and then he asked me, "Do you want a job?" Do boats float! Two weeks later I was on the way to one of the most secret testing facilities in the country, "Lake X!"

Lake Conlin~ once known as "Lake X"
By U.S. Fish and Wildlife Service Southeast Region (Uploaded by AlbertHerring) [CC BY 2.0 (http://creativecommons.org/licenses/by/2.0) or Public domain], via Wikimedia Commons

It was formally known as Lake Conlin, which was a 1300 plus acre lake in Osceola County, Florida. This is where, under the most intense security, the secrets to Kiekhaefer's enormous success were put to the test.

This highly secured property had a small hotel, an airstrip, mess tables, and trailers for us to live in. We worked hard, and soon became accustomed to long, grueling days, but the rewards were fantastic! There wasn't much time for recreation offsite, but there were great crew facilities on the property.

Once, my team partner, Paul and I were off for a full two days and we decided that we needed to just totally relax, so we would simply enjoy the employee facilities. We commenced early in the morning to take a couple of the specially made pedal bikes, similar to today's mountain bikes; they were designed to attach to a two-wheeled pull trailer that would accommodate a large cooler. This was much appreciated by the "travel restricted" staff. Besides, with as hard as we were working, who wanted to go partying?

We were each heavily loaded as we hit the dirt pathway that led off to a private camping area. When we arrived, the place was completely empty, so we picked one of the small tent-like cubicles and settled in. Taking out a couple of hammocks, we were soon gently swaying barefooted and drinking beer. This employee park even had a well-cared for swimming beach. They really pampered us, and I was still pinching myself to see if I was dreaming!

Later on, we built a fire in our spot's fire pit using the chopped wood from a large stack of split logs, and soon we had demolished a lot of groceries and beer. After the sun had set it was still hot and humid, so Paul and I headed for our private beach. The moon was bright enough to leave the flashlights behind, which we soon learned was a mistake.

We had been only a few minutes in the water when there came a large splash throwing water 10 feet high and covering us with a sudden chill as the water was a lot cooler than the air.

With chattering teeth, we looked inland for the jokester. Seeing nothing, I called out some crazy challenge and Paul yelled along with me when there came a large log flying from behind the bushes that were back from the beach. The log was clearly visible in the bright moonlight, and it landed right alongside me with another huge splash. I pushed through the water to grab it as a defensive weapon, but after I grasped it, it was too heavy for me to lift out of the water! I could raise it up finally with both hands, but I couldn't even do more than lift it up and I dropped it back. That's when I knew it wasn't one of our own people playing a prank; this was seriously dangerous!

Lake Conlin ~ once known as "Lake X"
By U.S. Fish and Wildlife Service Southeast Region (Uploaded by AlbertHerring) [CC BY 2.0
(http://creativecommons.org/licenses/by/2.0) or Public domain], via Wikimedia Commons

Paul splashed over to my side pointing at the shore and said that he saw the culprit, but it looked like some kind of a large orangutan like there were at the zoo, only taller and larger than a man. We decided to postpone our swim and get back to the security of our camp, and since no more missiles were thrown our way, we ran straight to camp; me grabbing the army shovel and Paul the hatchet.

There was no sign of any animal, but our camp had been torn apart! The two packs of hot dogs were gone, there were cookies and potato chips scattered, beer bottles strewn about as it evidently couldn't figure out how to open them, and the strangest thing was, that the two huge bags of ice cubes were missing from both coolers.

We searched the area with our flashlights and after we had trampled out any possible sign around the fire pit, we explored in ever widening circles and finally found some large tracks that had to be the creature's tracks. It had rained heavily the day before and these were the only tracks other than our own. We followed the trail across the narrow peninsula, carrying the shovel and hatchet for defense, and we were now less afraid than curious. After about 200 feet, the sand turned to marsh again and our tracking ability ended in ankle deep, swampy water, and when Paul said the word, "alligator," I was on dry land 10 feet from the water in two seconds flat!

There were many nods of familiarity back at our main quarters the next evening, and our story wasn't laughed at as we had expected. It seemed that we were about the only ones who hadn't been aware of this "swamp ape," as they referred to it back then; along with "swamp Sasquatch!"

In those days, everything that happened at "Lake X" was strictly confidential and all of us were sworn to secrecy under a legal contract, and we sure weren't about to lose our huge bonuses only to be laughed at for having seen the Bigfoot!

Dennis S. ~ Toronto, Ontario

19 BIGFOOT AWAKENS

My great friend, Frank, joined me in fulfilling the one item on my bucket list that I needed help on; and that was to explore the south side of the Rogue River wilderness area in Oregon.

Gary, I remember you from when you were president of the Josephine County Historical Society and the information you gave me from your archives helped to locate the hidden gold mine, for which I cannot thank you enough; thanks also to Kerby Jackson! The Sasquatch I ran into was not part of our research, so I'll fill you in for your upcoming book. I know that you will protect my identity, as my wife really became worried when the local news media got wind of our experience from the Sheriff's department, but Frank and I denied everything and said the rafter got the story wrong; ha! I don't think our new sheriff had any desire to pursue it anyway, as he still doesn't have enough staff.

The Rogue River just past the Grave Creek boat launch

We launched our raft at the Grave Creek boat launch and on the way down the river; we stopped at the Black Bar Lodge. As you know, the case was never solved, but the original owner, Mr. Black, was mysteriously murdered as so many, many others have been killed along this river. We asked a few questions about certain areas they were known to have information about. We made camp not far from there on the south side of the Rogue and re-read the map that you had sketched out some suggestions on. I turned out to be spot-on!

Grave Creek Rapids

Along our way the next morning, we passed many areas where there were obvious signs of man's search for gold, although there were no souvenirs from the old times, as in those days, everything they brought in was used until it no longer had any value, as to bring in supplies to the miners was a major undertaking, so tools were used until there was nothing left. Plus the fact that during the major flood, back when the waters running through there were like 36 feet higher than normal and destroyed so many years of this area's history that can never be recovered or even recorded!

The wild and scenic Rogue River

The second day, we continued downriver 'til that time of day when the afternoon shadows begin to camouflage the details in the high cliffs when we pulled in at a unique spot where there was a sandy area between two massive boulders. This spot appealed to us from a distance, because our approach from upriver indicated that there was a sandy depression with a scattering of trees behind where we landed, so we secured the raft and headed up and around the large rocks, and there before us, was a beautiful spot amongst the willows to pitch our tent.

We saw an indentation that when uncovered, proved to be a circle of rocks that at one time had seen use as a fire pit. Once we scraped the sand away, it was very large and from the long dead coals around the area, we figured it had seen a lot of use over a long period of time; kind of a permanent camp. Another indicator was all around this area there were signs of trees that had once been chopped off and new growth had sprouted from the sides, that with Frank's knowledge of trees from 30 years working for the U.S. Forestry Department, he felt this may have been a main camp for one of the Chinese mines. They pretty much controlled this entire area and relentlessly guarded it, and nobody even challenged them. They must have had total control of about a half a mile, which in those times was huge!

It was rapidly growing dark as the sun retreated from this deep, dark canyon. We saw a couple of deer on a path across the river about 100 feet above us. As we utilized the fire pit, the chilling air was mitigated by our pleasant campfire, using our approved camp stove (no open fires this time of year).

We awoke early after a deep sleep and prepared to get on our way downriver when a small group of "late to retire" bats caught our eyes as they retreated to the still dark cliffs behind us. The sun had barely indicated that it would be up soon, but we both thought it strange that those bats headed to what we had thought was a bare cliff.

Frank and I agreed that since this was a trip to explore the area for old mines, and we were only a short ways from the mine you and I had discussed at the Historical Society library; that we'd better take a look as long as we were here to see if the bats knew something that we didn't.

We further secured our raft and hid our supplies behind a distant sand dune, and taking canteens and army shovels, and my old army .45 Colt pistol and Frank's ancient Iver Johnson .22, off we went.

This canyon was absolutely deceptive; what had seemed to be the end of the cliff turned out to be a short ridge between the river and the cliffs beyond, but it made it appear that the high wall was part of this ridge. We had assumed that it ended in another couple hundred feet, but that turned out not to be the case; as we walked down the sand dune it led around the narrow ridge and around the other side was like another canyon larger than a city block. Here the floor flattened out, and as we curved slightly to our left; nothing! Only a sparse forest of pine trees ranging from around four feet high to well over 100 feet, but no gold mine! Under the far side of the cliff opposite us, a small waterfall trickled into a wide pool and met with others that all drained into a steadily flowing creek that fed into the Rogue River just past our campsite.

We decided to continue downriver when our eyes were diverted by a stunning bald eagle floating magnificently overhead, and I was suddenly reminded of the bats. I blurted out, "What about the bats?" Frank stopped in his tracks and we looked at each other, and he said he'd forgotten about them. We couldn't remember how many there were, but there had been a lot of them and they had to be going somewhere very near here, because they were circling around, as I've seen bats do when taking turns entering their caves. It reminded me of the time I was exploring in Ecuador, and it seemed they'd never stop coming!

Now, I am not in any sense knowledgeable of bats, but I have always believed that they spent their days in a dark place. All my life when I hear about bats, I form a mental picture of them hanging upside down in caves. I know that the Oregon Caves are said to stretch over twenty-plus miles and there have been reports by friends of mine who work at our national monument that have told me they believe that these bats travel the entire length of the caves all the way to Marble Mountain near Selma, Oregon; that's 20 to 30 miles of caves! Maybe there were caves here that had never been found, or maybe the bats were nesting in old mines.

As we sat with coffee cups in hand, Frank and I decided to spend the rest of the day relaxing and lying around camp. Then after we finished a day of tossing stones at sticks we threw in the river, napping in the comfort of another beautiful day, we carefully and quietly made our way through the willow trees until we neared the ridge that lay between us and those distant cliffs. We got as high as we dared on the side of the dunes where we could still be in the willows, but also see most of the cliff face.

Aware that the bats usually become active in the Rogue River Canyon's depths well before sunset, we kept our eyes on the walls ahead until finally Frank spotted one. Then another bat appeared from roughly the same area and soon we were able to determine that they seemed to be emerging from a place up and to our far left, around the corner from where we stopped before, and there was still enough natural light to see, and since we were in an area already in the darkening shadows, we ventured around the cliff and kept near the wall. We hadn't gone a couple hundred feet before we abruptly turned back to our right and the area the bats were emerging from was directly above us maybe a hundred feet.

We were both carefully walking and watching the ever increasing flow of bats; there must have been 20 by now. We were about to question how we'd ever get way up on that ridge when we practically fell on the answer. There before us were steps cut into the cliff's wall! They were obviously man-made and crudely chiseled, but functional. They were almost entirely covered at the bottom with sand and nearly invisible against the cliff until one was underneath and looking up. These chiseled steps were narrow and around a foot apart heading up to the shelf above. There on the ground near the bottom step, was a practically rusted out head of a pick. I cannot describe the exuberance that overcame me by this discovery! Not just because we found an old pick head, but that plus the steps was all it took. This was maybe the key to one of the legendary, early mines that were both known and rumored to have been great producers of gold!

We headed back to camp while we could still find it in the ever-darkening twilight and made plans to be up before dawn to be in position when the bats returned home. We were up early the next morning and hastily made breakfast enough to last for a long day, and packed water, a couple of snacks, army shovels, a small pick, a chisel and hand mall, and of course our sidearms. We made our way by moonlight and an occasional quick flash of a flashlight beam and we were soon back at the cliff. When we reached the steps, it was still very dark there, so we sat down to wait.

It wasn't long until we saw a faint shadow coming in, and to our surprise, the bat flew in about 50 feet above our heads. Then another, and soon it was like the New York subway from my childhood; a constant flow of small bats, all pinpointing the area like a beam!

With enough light to see, we began to carefully climb onto each step, and brushing the sand off the next one with our hands and army shovel, we made good time even though the sand on the steps was hard packed, not at all loose as we had expected, which was a sign that the sand had been there a very long time. Within 20 minutes of making our way up these narrow cuts (the steps were about the width of a brick), we came out on a flat shelf and we both walked to our left where the bats had all flowed, and just around a large boulder was a tunnel! It was completely hidden from below, as once we were back a few steps; we couldn't see the valley any longer. At this ledge, the walkway widened considerably as we entered the darkness.

It was definitely man-made, but it was more of a widening of a huge crack running into the cliff's face. We started in, then as we proceeded deeper with our camp lights, the tunnel curved very slightly into the mountain as if the miners had been following a gold vein, and every once in a while, we could see flecks of gold, and one fairly large, about 1/8 inch wide streak, that was too far above our heads, or I'd have tried to pick it out; darn! The tunnel continued into the mountain, and we kept hearing the fluttering of the bats whose home we were invading. I took a photo with my phone that I have attached.

All of a sudden, we heard a thumping as though something big was running further in the tunnel, and instinctively, my hand was on my pistol and my heart was beating so loud I could no longer hear the footfalls, and then something ran right into me, or should I say over and through me like a huge linebacker; it truly stomped me to the ground. I gasped out all the air in my lungs when it ran over me and I heard Frank yell as he went down also. Then, we both gained our feet and rushed after the creature without thinking!

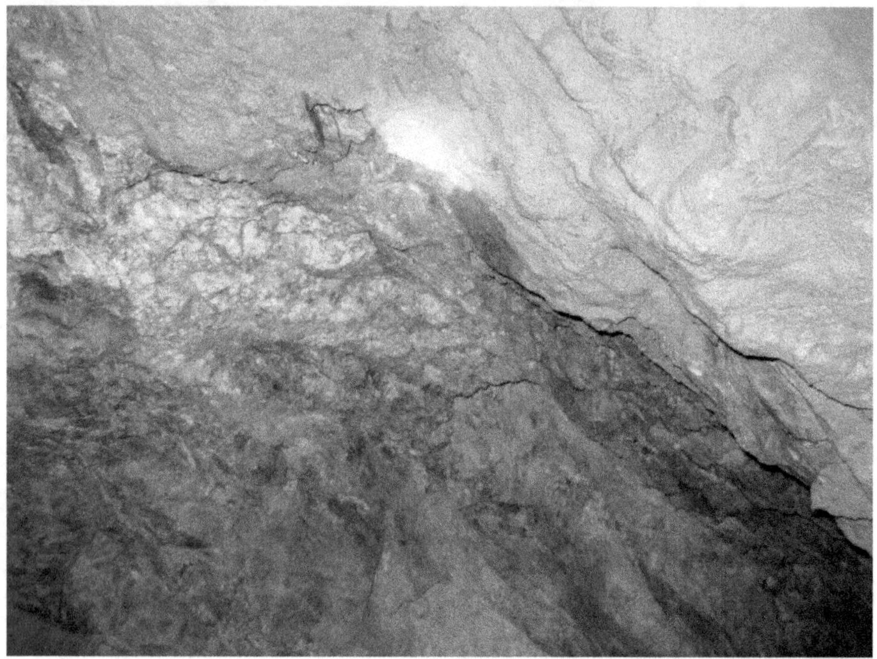
By L.H.

We both realized that it wasn't a bear, because we weren't clawed, and since it ran, it gave us the courage to chase it, and within seconds we emerged onto the plateau, and in the morning sun, we could clearly see a large, brown beast looking like a huge, shaggy ape; only it ran more straight up like a human. Its fur was flowing as it ran, unlike other forest animals whose fur was more close to their bodies. Its hands seemed to be very large, but the feet weren't as long as I would have thought for that size of creature.

The animal was headed for a large gap in between this cliff and another one ahead, and just as it prepared to leap into a dark forested area, it turned back toward us and put both hands in the air above its massive head and made a tearing gesture like one would make tearing down a paper sign or something; then it was gone!

Both Frank and I knew instantly what it was, because a lot of our friends have had encounters with the Sasquatch, but they were mostly sightings and almost running into them on roads and such. This was the real thing!

This was the very first one that Frank and I had ever seen, and I was surprised to find myself shaking all over like I was in shock. Frank joined me as I was recovering on the stone steps. You talk about an experience! We stayed around up there for quite a while, but there were no other signs of tunnels or caves, but there was enough brush and grasses in the tunnel that we reckoned this Bigfoot must have slept there often, and one side corner was full of still-green pine branches, so maybe that was its permanent home. Maybe sometime we'll go back there after our retirement, as this was absolutely the greatest! We have talked about bringing metal detectors and a short ladder, as I have not forgotten that gold streak!

Unfortunately, neither of us dares to reveal this episode, because we are on the board of directors for an investment company and it wouldn't look too good to our stockholders for us to be seeing monsters! Anyway, thanks for at least letting our experience be told. I have your new address, so if we get back in there again, I'll let you know; it will be with a lot more equipment, and a camera! Maybe you could join us?*

T. H. ~ Medford, Oregon

Publishers note: I'm ready to go gentlemen; let me know when, and we'll both head for Oregon!

20 BIGFOOT'S GOLD

After our careers teaching in California, we retired to live our dream in Southern Oregon. My wife Teri and I had spent the last several years studying everything about our new home and first on our bucket list was to locate a place to find gold and then file a real gold claim! Filing a claim is relatively easy as long as you can show proof of some gold and the particular spot of ground is unclaimed. We pictured the perfect retirement; earning extra money on our own claim. Since childhood, I had often daydreamed about this scenario; I have always been so fascinated with the gold rush of 1849!

So here we were, all settled in and having researched, bought supplies, GPS unit, maps, and having spent hours talking with old-timers in the area. We headed out to our chosen site near the Little Chetco River in the mountains east of our home in Brookings, Oregon. We wanted to find a place not too far away so we could spend time on our new hobby. We had been following the ongoing fight between the State of Oregon and the Federal Bureau of Land Management against a gold miner named Dave Rutan who legally owns a gold mine named Emily Camp. We were warned that the BLM would not make our dream easy, but we were determined.

Our thought was that if there was a successful mining operation nearby that as long as we put plenty of space between our claim and their legal boundaries that we could find another mountain stream to enjoy our small recreational claim at our leisure. Our quest was not to get rich; it was the thrill of actually finding gold on our own claim!

Once we had purchased a 4-wheel drive to get us through what these gold miners called roads, we proceeded to try to locate a way to go close to Mr. Rutan's mining operation and then turn off on another road, but to no avail. The entire area had burned in the huge Biscuit Fire in 2002, and any previously used logging roads had been blocked by huge, burned trees and the economics of profitably salvaging the timber had been repeatedly blocked by the government's attitude against any further use of the public land, so there were no roads to aid us to follow our dreams! Some of the forests in areas around this Chetco area were not touched, and therefore we figured we could at least get close, but the BLM beat us to it and closed off all the roads. The forests were a massive wasteland of monstrous burned and rotting trees crisscrossed on top of each other. In much of the mountains, the only larger animals that could even climb through the devastation were cougars and bobcats, and the deer stayed in the areas the fire skipped over.

Kalmiopsis Wilderness Area after the 2002 Biscuit Fire

It may seem rather naïve to have spent so much planning, and now here we were; no sooner had we started than we had seemingly been thwarted by Mother Nature! We had planned our entire venture, right down to dipping a gold pan into the water and picking out nuggets! Now, we were facing insurmountable odds against even finding a piece of this mountain to file a claim on.

The main road to Emily Camp was blocked and locked with enough "Keep Out" signs that we never got close. We had not anticipated that the roads shown on the forestry maps would be impassable, so we set about exploring for a spot where we could make it through.

We went home to reconnoiter and our research showed it may be possible to approach the area from the top down. So we drove around to the town of Selma, Oregon and followed the Illinois River on the other side of the mountains until we were able to cross the river and climb the winding dirt roads up into the beautiful, unburned, green forests until we reached the trailhead that we had used previously, and day-hiked to the absolutely stunning Babyfoot Lake! Passing the trailhead we followed the 4X4 road until it became little more than a deeply rutted trail. At that point, our maps and GPS directions indicated that we were at a location roughly on top of the mountain above Emily Camp and close to the birthplace of the Little Chetco River.

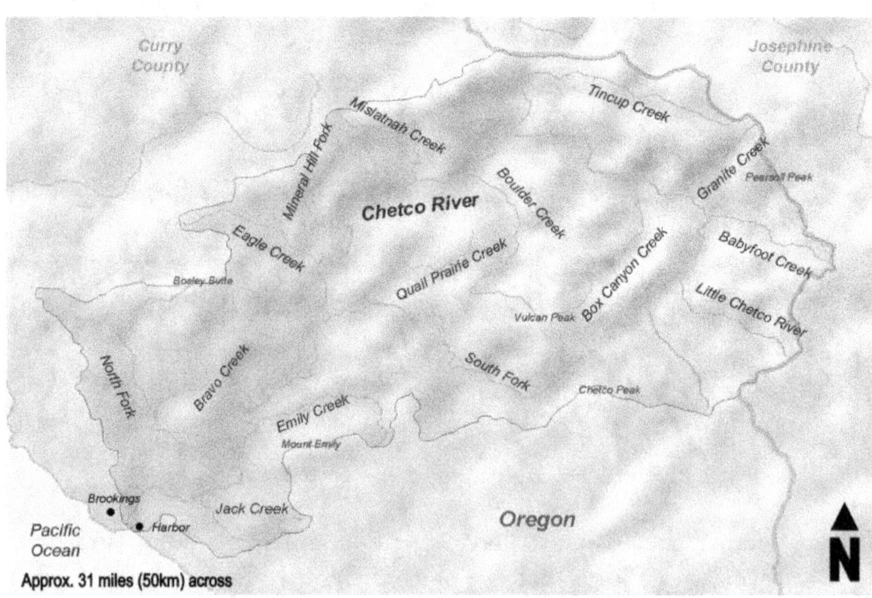

By Demis Map Server, Little Mountain 5 [CC BY-SA 3.0
(https://creativecommons.org/licenses/by-sa/3.0) or GFDL
(http://www.gnu.org/copyleft/fdl.html)], via Wikimedia Commons

With our packs heavily laden and our belts carrying all sorts of gear including the revolvers we were each packing. Even though we did not anticipate any dangers, it sure adds a huge degree of comfort. Hiking down a steep mountain was certainly a great deal more difficult than we had ever imagined, and we spent a solid two days fighting our way down through some pretty rough terrain.

We would sleep until the first glow of dawn and then push on. On the third day, suddenly without warning, we emerged onto the remnants of an ancient, poorly graded, but obvious road. Then within 100 feet was a cabin. A very old, but intact cabin; it was obviously abandoned, the glass still unbroken in the windows and door unlocked. Funny how long things last when kept away from humans!

Babyfoot Lake, Kalmiopsis Wilderness Area

We shouted out a greeting, but were met only with the mocking call of a nearby raven and the ever constant mountain wind. Since this cabin had not been in the fire's path, we wondered what happened to its owner. We found clean dishes stacked neatly in the cupboards, flatware in drawers, and remnants of tattered wallpaper; lonely but still awaiting its owner's return.

Outside was what we thought was a one cylinder gasoline motor and an ingenious system where the water could be heated by the water pipe that stretched through the outdoor woodstove to heat the water that was then channeled into a water tank that supplied the tiled shower stall. Someone had just left and never returned; and this lonely cabin sat watching the small saplings growing in the road where their vehicles would never return. It was sad. We wished the house could talk, because someone had obviously lived here for a long time and it showed a great deal of love and caring.

Heading out, we began following the traces of the old road as it wound slightly down and around to our left when out of the pines, a huge piece of log came sailing out of nowhere and smashed into pieces against a pine tree I was walking by, sending pieces in all directions! Teri screamed and I drew my handgun from its holster and fired a shot into the dirt bank across the road. It had the desired effect as we could hear footsteps quickly receding into the brush.

After regaining our composure we continued down the faintly visible road until it disappeared completely. Off to our right we saw another road, only this time it was a single track where we could barely walk side by side.

Then surprisingly, there were signs of the path being well used and there were fresh cuts where saplings were broken or cut off. We were traveling at a slight angle upward and another hundred feet led us to an area where someone had built a rock and log bridge that enabled us to cross over the stream. Directly ahead was a large, oblong pond and at the other side, a narrow waterfall was cascading about 40 feet off a tall, gray cliff.

According to our GPS unit, we were less than two miles from the outer edge of the Emily Camp boundary, which meant we could most likely file a claim on this place if we were able to find a trace of gold. Someone had obviously been mining here long ago, as even the few cans we found were old and rusted, and new growth saplings dotted the area.

We decided to go a bit further, and as we curved around the cliff another 50 feet, there before us was a tunnel! It had been completely hidden, and here in a wide area were old, discarded barrels, timbers, boards and the trash and tin cans familiar to the old mines; at least those we had visited in California and Nevada on various vacations.

The tunnel showed signs of having once been boarded up, but over time the boards had fallen or been pulled aside by people or animals seeking shelter. The animal idea made the most sense, because neither of us could envision anyone hiking through this rugged country for recreation. Had we not had good reason, this terrain would be the last place to enter.

We dug into our packs for our fluorescent camp lanterns because they show such a lot of light, and leaving our packs at the entrance, we carefully entered the mine. By using both of our lights, we could see quite far ahead and the tunnel began to curve slowly, so from our limited knowledge, we made the assumption they had been following a vein of gold. This was quite common, as a golden streak may have kept going, and could be the only sign of gold in the whole rock wall. We knew from our research that miners followed the gold vein and they only stopped when it did!

We had gone another few feet when we heard a sound ahead of us that sounded like a grunt or maybe a sort of growl, and then in the next instant, we heard a ferocious snarl coming from the darkness and then a rock came careening off the wall and smacked me right in the ribs. I dropped to my knees in pain and Teri grabbed onto my arm just as two large animals pushed by us. We spun around to defend ourselves, but they kept going on a dead run as we knelt in stunned silence watching these huge creatures that looked like humans with very long legs; they were covered with brown fur and had huge feet. They ran around the curve and then nothing; not a sound! The only lingering evidence of their passing were some very large footprints, and a musty, skunk-like odor that was quite foul; however, as we discussed after this encounter, they probably had the same thoughts about us after three days of not showering!

We both saw them plainly, and since that experience and meeting, many of our new townsfolk; we have learned that these were the Sasquatch that our research had referred to as reclusive, but possibly dangerous humanoids that had been acknowledged in early journals of the gold miners going back to the California Gold Rush, and when the California gold fields were filled up, the gold hungry packs swung north. We returned by the GPS, doing some of the longest and most difficult climbing, and falling down, that either of us had ever experienced, and by the time this adventure was over, we were absolutely exhausted.

When we finally arrived back at our truck, we were convinced that even if we had filed a gold claim on one of the streams we had travelled across and around during our trip, simply working that hard to get in and out would be the worst retirement we could ever spend.

After listening to so many people in this area tell about their sightings and experiences with these Sasquatch, we're investigating a new pursuit. We should perhaps spend our efforts photographing and studying Bigfoot!

Pritchard and Teri Vandenburg ~ Brookings, Oregon

21 GOODBYE LAKESHORE VACATION

I hadn't been to the old family cabin for several years and I was looking forward to an entire two weeks all by myself. The company my parents paid to watch over it had done a good job and when I picked up the keys at their office, they reported no problems or repairs needed, and on their last monthly check the report showed nothing amiss. My parents seldom use the old place anymore, as the last time they were there Mom said a "monster" had chased her away from the lake and it had thrown sticks and rocks at her all the way up from the dock! She had asked me to check it out, because Dad wasn't in all that good of shape to make the trip anymore.

Locking the gate behind me, I slowly drove the rocky, rutted drive as it curved up and around the hill crest, and then it rapidly descended down the slope to what was the most private lake cabin in the area. In fact, this entire end of the two mile lake was surrounded by impassable swamps that denied access to anyplace on the entire third of this beautifully secluded lake; its depths were estimated to be up to 45 feet. The few other properties further away had to be reached by another roadway that required a 30 mile drive around the mountain and was accessible only by 4-wheel drive.

Parking directly in front of the cabin, I unlocked the oversized padlock securing the front door, and as I entered, I heard a loud screech which I thought to be a hawk, but then I thought back to Mom's comments about being chased by a monster. My father had not been with her that day as his health concerns had kept him home. I had wondered how my mother would have dared make the trip herself, but this cabin had very special memories for our family.

It was then I heard the screech again, so I stepped outside, but as I walked around the cabin, there wasn't a bird anywhere in the sky. As I returned to where I started, I heard something thump against the cabin and I quickly ran around to the back, and about 40 feet downhill toward the lake, I saw what appeared to be a tall, scrawny bear. Only it wasn't a bear; it was shaped more like a gaunt, long-haired orangutan! It was about six and a half to seven feet tall, with very short ears that came to a sharp point, maybe a short tail, but I couldn't see it well; it had very long arms, and its feet were long and narrow. I don't really recall its facial features so well, as I was keeping my eyes on the club-like stick in its right hand, and it held a softball sized rock in its left. The fingers seemed very long and its hands also seemed exceptionally large, and when I think hard, it may also have had long claws, but maybe I was imagining that.

Everything happened so fast the next thing I remember was barely ducking in time to keep from losing my entire face, as the beast had hurled the rock before I could even see and it caught me on the left cheek, and almost tore my ear off as it sent me sprawling! I was so much in shock that I don't even remember reacting, but all of a sudden I was brought back to reality by the huge blast from the revolver I was holding in my right hand.

Thank God for reflex action and my prior military experience, as I reacted automatically, and looking back I can truthfully say I'm here today because my mind and body did it without my help!

As my cloudy mind cleared, the animal had almost reached the bottom of the long hill. The last I saw it was entering the large, swampy pine forest that covered our entire end of the lake.

The rest of the night passed uneventfully, unless you can count three long screeches over an hours' time that could easily have been a screech owl as it could have been this Bigfoot guy, but my painfully swollen face and overactive imagination could not be swayed!

When I got home and told Mother about the incident, she called a Realtor friend and put the place up for sale. I concurred that I seriously doubted that the big-footed critter and I would ever form a bond of friendship, and I told her she was never going there again and either was I!

Howard Saxby ~ Twin Falls, Idaho

22 OUTGUNNED AT AN OREGON GOLD MINE

Hi Wendy, I hope you remember me. We met about four years ago when my husband and I were spending the summer near Galice, Oregon and searching for an ancient gold mine in the Mount Peavine area.   At that time you and your husband were considering publication of your hiking book. Well, we saw that you had published "Hiking Sasquatch Country," and we told you that we thought back then we had seen a Bigfoot prowling around our camp. So finally, I found the business card you gave me, so as I promised, here is our experience with what turned out to be the scariest time we've ever had! Please don't use our last name, because that summer was courtesy of a "no questions asked" two month emergency leave from hubby's company. Good thing his dad owns the place, so nobody dared ask questions anyway!

I remember when we last spoke, you had met quite a few residents of the Galice area who spoke openly about having had encounters with the Sasquatch, and you also said a lot of hikers in the county had also run into them. When we bought our supplies in Galice, the people in the rafting place acted like they had never heard of Sasquatch. Then as we asked more people we met, they told us that the local merchants were just worried about frightening tourists away, so they all cover up the reports. They don't make any money on hikers, so they keep the secret, but perhaps tourists should be warned!

Anyway, we drove to a place past Galice and up near where your Pyx gold mine was, and the folks at Galice told us you actually had bought the mine for the County Historical Society and that you raffled it off several years ago. Too bad, we'd have bought some tickets. So we found the area indicated by your hand-drawn map, and after many wrong turns, we found the trail had been covered by brush evidently pushed up by the road graders. We cleared away enough to get the Jeep through, but after another 100 feet we were blocked by a huge pine that had fallen right across the road. Evidently it lost a battle with lightning.

It hadn't taken that long to get there from Galice, so we took our time and set up our tent behind some huge boulders off of the old road where we were surrounded by a beautiful pine forest with views of the whole mountainous region. It is absolutely stunning up there!

A view from Mount Peavine

We got camp set up and took a canteen and our handguns and off we went, climbing the old mining road (if you could call it a road).

The records that we had indicated that there was another mine called the "Bunker Hill" nearby, but the photocopy said something about it having been closed by the BLM. We had been informed by some customers we met at the Armadillo Mining Shop in Grants Pass that the BLM had the nasty habit of blowing up and sealing every old mine they could, so after seeing the evidence of a massive rockslide and old broken timbers all over the place, we sort of got the idea that maybe my husband's uncle's old gold mine had met similar fate. Maybe that was why the road was blocked.

It didn't really matter all that much, because Uncle Jake had warned us before we left. Besides that, he hadn't bothered to renew his claim for years, because when he moved to California, the law's requirement of two weeks of "claim improvement" per year wasn't feasible any longer, so we would have been shocked if it was still in any condition to be claimed again. If we did locate it, we had decided to go ahead and file on it since we were planning to move up to Medford and we actually would have the time to spend vacations digging for gold

One of the many abandoned roads on Mount Peavine

We spent the first night enjoying the cold mountain breeze in front of a rugged fire pit constructed of a large half circle of boulders. The next day was spent searching the area with the aid of our GPS, and we finally found where the coordinates were exact. A huge area of boulders and a lot of timbers, many broken and bent pieces of steel, a field of wire, metal pipes, old tires, and sections of twisted rails from what must have been for small ore cars, and a lot of junk is what remained of Uncle Jake's mine. So much for our mental picture of what a gold mine should look like.

Returning downhill to camp brought a new surprise; the doors on the Jeep stood open, our tent was listing to the side; food, blankets and clothes were scattered around like a drunken FBI agent who was looking for evidence had been here! Nothing was broken, but everything seemed to have been inspected. It didn't take long to straighten up, but the ice chest had sat open long enough to have lost about half of the ice, but otherwise, no big deal.

Entrance to a gold mine shut down by the BLM on Mount Peavine

Or so we thought; our spare revolver was gone! It had been under the tarp between our sleeping bags. The gun was gone, but the case it had been in was still there. It was only a .22 caliber nickel plated Browning, so we weren't worried about the cost, but if some kid had taken it; we could all be in trouble!

In order to at least justify the trip and get some value out of our vacation, we decided to keep the campsite, and there was a tiny stream nearby so we settled in, cleaned up the place and hauled a few boards and small timbers over, and soon our camp looked good; like the ones you see in the movies.

There we were, nestled back in the pines, benches and cleared areas covered with pine branches looked like green carpeting; it made a peaceful setting to read some of the books we had saved for this trip.

Then, the third night brought us regrets. About an hour after sunset, with the sky still light, but darkness having surrounded our area, a large rock came soaring from the forest and landed in the center of our camp. Within seconds, another even larger one hit the ground and rolled directly into our fire pit, scattering coals and ashes four feet away. After beating out the fire with pine branches and yelling obscenities at whoever had done this, we heard the most gosh awful howling and screaming from directly over the small hill toward the mine!

In answer, I aimed my pistol at the dirt bank by the old mine adit and fired two rounds. The roar was deafening in this sheltered clearing, and we heard what we knew must have been some kind of animals running up the hill, and then, there they stood; visible against the twilight sky were two ape-like animals staring down at us from the rise. We heard a muffled snarl, due to our ears still ringing from the gunshots, and then a kind of snort from the beasts, and then they were gone!

We figured that we had just met the Sasquatch that we had heard so much of, ever since we had met you folks way back when, and we had become interested. By daylight, we couldn't make out more than a couple of very light footprints where these critters had stood, but they were still pronounced just enough in the morning to guess them to be a bit over 18 inches long. Long enough for us to end our vacation on that mountain!

I do hope that whichever one of these Sasquatch stole my gun never learns how to use it. When I turned in my insurance claim, my agent advised me to simply forget it. He said something along the lines of, "Nobody, me included, will ever believe you lost a gunfight to Sasquatch!"

Jean and Tom ~ Medford, Oregon

23 SHOULD SASQUATCH NEED A HUNTING LICENSE FOR PEOPLE?

I have sat on this story for three years now 'til a buddy of mine mentioned your books and I then I found that "Sasquatch Watch" Facebook site, so my wife is figuring out how to load this story up so we can send it to you and find out if you can use it.

I came face to face with a very large and scary Sasquatch four years ago during deer hunting season. I was up in the coast range where I have filled my tag seven out of eight years. This is the only time I really get to escape in the forests I love so much, and it is a welcome respite from my constantly being in demand as a caregiver in a large nursing facility. Even my wife is happy to hear my stories about hunting adventures instead of the constant problems I bring home from work each day. This time gives her time to herself as well.

As I have done for all but one year, I take my best friend Vince with me as he shares my interests and he's also a crack shot. Vince always fills his tag! It was the third day of the season, and as usual, Vince and I go so far down a new trail, and at a certain point, we separate and pick our own post alongside one of three mountain meadows about a half mile from each other.

On this particular day, we had separated and I was about a quarter of a mile along where the path ran alongside a small creek, when all of a sudden a man came staggering around a huge pine tree where the trail turned, and upon seeing me, he let out a loud "No!" Then the energy just seemed to leave his body and he sank to his knees; exhausted. I gave him some water and a granola bar, and I squatted alongside him until he wolfed the bar down and was finally able to talk.

I won't give his name, because he was too embarrassed over what he was about to tell me, and besides that, he had called in sick at work to make this trip. This experience must have been his payback!

It turned out that he said he was hunting on the flat area about 800 yards down the trail when a large bear-like animal rushed out of the forest and knocked him to the ground. His rifle went flying off his shoulder and into the steep gulch beyond. When he recovered enough to get to his feet, the animal was standing there glaring at him with what he said were fierce, reddish eyes; he said they glowed like hot coals! The animal fit the description of the Bigfoot sketches everyone is familiar with to a tee! Then he said the creature started coming toward him and he twisted around as he scrambled to his feet, but his right foot sank to his ankle in a deep mud hole in the trail and he had to grab his right knee with both hands and lunged with all his might to get his leg freed from the hole, but his boot was stuck solid.

View of the Coast Range Mountains from Saddle Mountain in Clatsop County, Oregon
By brx0 [CC BY-SA 2.0 (https://creativecommons.org/licenses/by-sa/2.0)], via Wikimedia
Commons

With the beast coming toward him, he didn't dare to try to retrieve it, and as his feet hit solid ground again, his sock also came off, but he was scared to death this hairy beast would kill him, so he ran as fast as he could, trying to avoid projecting rocks and sticks, but he said with every step his foot was screaming in torture, and as I poured water from my canteen over his bloody foot, he winced in what had to be excruciating pain, from his sudden ghostly, white complexion!

He said finally his body could go no further and he fully expected to die, so he just gave up and collapsed. He said he knew the ape-man would tear him to pieces, but when nothing happened by the time he was able to force a look back, the beast was gone. Then he said he risked sitting flat and looked around carefully watching for an attack, and he had to address the horrendous pain in his foot. The entire outer layer of skin was gone and the blood was flowing continually. There was no way he could go back to try to extricate his boot from the mud hole as he feared he would be killed and maybe eaten by the Sasquatch, or "devil ape" as he called it then, but it didn't follow. He thought it probably sensed or heard me coming, but I don't seriously believe it would have hurt him. The Sasquatch I've heard about do not ever attack humans.

Coast Range Mountains looking west toward the Pacific Ocean
By Loren Kerns [CC BY-SA 2.0 (https://creativecommons.org/licenses/by-sa/2.0)], via Flickr

I looked down at his foot to see how I could help; he pleaded with me to just leave it. He had used his knife to cut his right trouser leg off above the knee and he had wrapped his foot and ankle with the cloth and tied it with cords from his backpack and taped it hard over with the first aid kit tape.

He thanked me when I escorted him to his pickup which was about an eighth of a mile around the curve ahead. I told him I'd retrieve his boot for him, but he said to leave it as he didn't want the memory, and when he got to his truck, he'd be gone from this damned mountain, throw the other boot away and try to forget about his horrible experience. He said he'd made his last hunt!

I returned to where I had found him and resumed my hunt. As I continued down the gradually dropping trail, I could see in the wet dirt and clay the scrapes where the man more or less dragged his wounded foot, but it was about a quarter of a mile until I came across a muddy hole with a hiking sock on the edge of the mud and the heel of a hiking boot poking out of the mud.

I left it as it was and for the rest of the hunt, my partner and I kept a watchful eye out for the "devil ape," but he obviously didn't want any part of more humans invading his mountain.

Glenn ~ Astoria, Oregon

24 THE FAMILY ON GRAYBACK MOUNTAIN

I have a placer claim on one of the many creeks on Grayback Mountain in Josephine County, Oregon. I don't want to be any more specific than that, because I'd rather not share my identity, but you can call me Jake.

One late October day another miner called me and told me he'd seen four men on my claim. He didn't confront them because he was outnumbered, besides he's an "old-timer" like me. My wife and I were packing up our trailer and getting ready to head for Yuma, Arizona for the season; the wet and foggy winters of Southern Oregon chill her to the bone. I decided I'd better investigate, because I don't want people stealing my meager supply of "color!"

One of the many small creeks on Grayback Mountain

The next morning I was up early, and while she finished prepping the trailer, I headed for my claim. It's not a very long drive, about 20 miles, and then it only takes an hour of hiking to reach it. When I got there, it was surely a mess! The trespassers had torn my claim signs from the trees and had been digging in the creek. They had left trash all over the place and had even made a fire pit.

I had brought my military shovel with me, so I got to work repairing the damage to the area and removed all signs of the fire pit. I didn't have anything to put the trash in, so I buried it with the idea I'd pack it out when I returned in the late spring. I didn't want any hunters or hikers to stumble upon the area and think it suitable for a campsite. As I was trying to obliterate all traces of anyone having been there, it started to rain heavy and the temperature was dropping quickly.

I hurried up the mountain a ways to find some shelter. There are several small caves and rocky overhangs in this area, and I was hoping to find one nearby that wasn't occupied by a black bear. By the time I found one and ducked inside, I was soaking wet. It was pretty dark and I didn't hear the sounds of any critters, so I turned on my flashlight and slowly looked around the enclosure. I planned to build a small fire and dry out a bit before I hastened back to my truck.

A small cave on Grayback Mountain

There back in the far corner was a mother Sasquatch and a very young infant at her breast! Being so familiar with the mountains of Southern Oregon, I immediately knew what I was looking at; this area is well known for being the home of Bigfoot although I had never seen any myself before now. Momma looked every bit as surprised as I was and she tightly wrapped her arms around her baby to protect it and snarled at me with nasty looking fangs and reddish eyes that were like lasers! Before she could react any further, I quickly backed out of the shelter not wanting to cause her any more stress and also knowing that Papa must not be too far away.

I moved hastily back down the mountain and stopped to look back after about 200 yards. Sure enough, here comes Mr. Sasquatch with a small deer over his shoulder. I believe I got out of there just in time! Before losing sight of the cave, I looked back once more to see the big Sasquatch standing guard outside the entrance. He needn't have worried; I surely wasn't going back in there again!

You may be surprised at how casually I report this, but long ago, I became acquainted with Sasquatch. About 12 years back, five other claim owners up and down the creek and I aided in keeping their identity a secret. We rather enjoyed having the big guys around. They make really good neighbors by keeping other animals like coyotes away. The wife sends me with stuff from the garden in season to leave out for them. There's a couple of big caves on one claim up above, and the claim owner lets 'em live in there.

By the time I got home I was so wet and miserable and came down with a nasty cold the next morning. We had to postpone our trip south for a few days, and it was so nice to get down here into the warm sunshine.

It's now late January and I've been seriously thinking I should sell my placer claim to a younger man and relocate to Arizona permanently; I know Jane would readily agree. I understand that there are a lot of lode mines on public land in Mojave County; so maybe the wife and I will take a ride up to Lake Havasu and check it out.

Jake ~ Murphy, Oregon

25 A SIGHTING GOES FROM POSSIBLE TO ABSOLUTELY CONVINCED

I have reversed my "on the fence" theory about our Sasquatch encounter of years back. I noted this incident in our first book "Hiking Sasquatch Country," but since it was strictly a hiking book, my sighting and our experience first appeared in "They Saw Sasquatch" which came about from stories we began to receive from others who wished to have a way to tell their stories.

Over time, I have become even more convinced that I actually saw the real thing. This motivated me to dig out my field notes, and as I read my own words, I found additional evidence that I had previously ignored. Now, after reading the information sent by our many contributors who have experienced similar incidents, they have convinced me that I can officially conclude that, "Sasquatch saw me," even though I had the camera and the photo was blurred, it was the real thing! Thinking back, I can remember why the photo was blurred; because the beast was looking into the lens and I was the one shaking!

This hike took place in one of Oregon's most heavily worked area of wall to wall, or should I say "valley to valley" gold claims. Here on the famous Briggs Creek, there was not an inch of space between where one claim ended and another began.

Remnants of mining equipment along the Briggs Creek trail

The entire topography of peaks and valleys are pocked with evidence of hydraulic mining where the huge nozzles or "giants" concentrated the built-up pressure of the water to a force capable of completely eroding entire hillsides of gravel, trees and rocks down the mountain, and then channeling the dirt and sand through the network of sluice boxes where the process rapidly reduced the material down to considerable smaller rocks, and finally gold; tons of it!

Hiking along these permanent traffic lanes where miners, mules and horses left lasting roadways gives the imagination just cause to reflect on the historical significance that killed hundreds of years of forest growth in only a few, fast-paced years.

As we hiked once more through this area after we had decided to write our hiking guide so others could enjoy what we had come to love. As we researched old mining records, miner's diaries and various newspaper articles dating back to the beginning of Josephine County, we found a creature that had occasionally been noted in early records, but largely ignored in historical texts for fear of ridicule as was briefly noted on a few old diaries and personal journals kept by the few miners who could read and write. Besides, the old timers were busy enough guarding their claims without getting hunters looking for new sport, and as one miner so succinctly noted; I bet the damn things taste as bad as they look!

The washed away hillside shows evidence of early hydraulic mining

About the third time we dropped into this rapidly descending valley we had our miniature schnauzers along; not for protection, but to alert the entire valley that we were coming. We often wonder how much we might have discovered if we had been stealthy, but when we started hiking, we had no knowledge of the existence of a species of animal so mysterious and secretive that it lives among us with only rare mention. We also assumed our dogs barked so much because of excitement, but perhaps there had been more to it!

Since we began collecting and publishing our stories, we found that a majority of our contributors have sat on their sightings and experiences out of fear of ridicule and not knowing who to tell. Many of our submitters communicate such excitement and relief at finally being able to share their encounters with such an amazing animal!

Wendy with our two alarm systems

Our personal experience on this hike began about a half a mile from our jump off point at the Sam Brown Campground. It started with a noise in the brush off to the left side between us and Briggs Creek. Assuming it to be one of many forest dwellers, deer, squirrel, rabbit or one of twenty possibilities, we ignored it and the dogs only yapped a little, but they do that upon seeing butterflies also.

This terrain was clear on the well-established trail, but on both sides, the thick brush was impassable; at least by hikers with leashes and dogs that invariably go every direction but straight. After a short ways, the dogs abruptly changed their behavior and they now began pulling hard on their leashes as we continued down the path and they were walking straight ahead, but they were continually looking to their left and uttering low growls. The fact that they were going straight should have alerted us right away!

With Wendy holding both leashes, I attempted to penetrate the brush in the direction of the creek where something was really bothering the "kids," but it was no-go. I couldn't see trying to go any further than the two feet of progress I made into the undrerbrush, as the blackberries will shred a person to pieces, and I was also confronted with some strange bushes with long thorns every inch or so and I had no desire to go into their world!

Whatever was out there occasionally made noise so it seemed to still be walking parallel to us as we continued our descent into the valley. The animal was not at all stealthy like a deer, and besides that, I've tramped through enough forests in a dozen states, and few have ever been so thick as this one, so I couldn't see why anything would even attempt to travel through there, except for some dummy trying to write a hiking book!

Wendy and I had pictured it being a deer, but we were surprised it was so noisy. We couldn't think of any wild animal that would follow a human in this part of the country. Obviously from its noisy passage, it was not afraid of us, but our dogs were afraid of it! We were not worried because I was carrying a handgun that was more than enough against any animal in this area except a bear, which only poses a danger when cubs are about, and this was not the right time of year for them. We thought about a human, but no man was capable of such stealth or could be crazy enough to try it.

As we went on our way, the noises in the brush continued, and though we were constantly reminded that we were being paced, we also knew that it couldn't have been human! On occasion, I took the time to push and claw to bend saplings and thorn bushes aside to go into the brush, but to no avail. There were no trees that I could climb for observation, as the only large trees were anywhere from 40 feet to over 100 feet high with no lower branches in this beautifully mature forest.

We were curious enough to keep our attention specifically on this creature and we were aware that we would soon solve this mystery, due to having hiked here before. We knew that eventually the trail that we were on would turn sharply left and cross Briggs Creek and continue up the mountain, and when that happened, the mystery would end with us meeting face to face with this animal. As we approached the point where the trail began curving, the noises suddenly ceased, and our footfalls were the only sounds other than the rippling of the creek as it picked up speed as the slope steepened. We had anticipated being able to finally meet whatever had been keeping pace with us as we walked stealthily as we could on the trail and it walked through absolute brush. No such luck! We purposely went fast for the last several yards and stopped abruptly on a higher knoll in a more open area and fully expected to meet maybe a cougar or coyote, but no; nothing! So, we waded through the creek and continued on the path as it climbed up and around the next mountain. Even as we climbed the steep slope on the other side of the creek where we could see a long ways back, there was no sign of any animal!

We were headed for an old cabin a local miner friend had told us about, but we had not made as good a time as we had hoped due to too many stops to identify our follower, so we finally turned around and headed back the way we had come. Besides that, we had remembered that we had heard the old cabin had recently collapsed.

We had forgotten about the earlier incident, but as we re-crossed Briggs Creek, we had not gone more than 50 yards when the strange noises began again, to our right this time; still between the trail and the creek. We surmised that whatever it was, had simply stopped and remained there until we returned; talk about unnerving!

Now the dogs began growling and the hair on their backs echoed the hair on the back of my neck as the sounds of this creature walking through the brush repeated. As we wound our way along the trail, we neared an open spot on our right that we had passed the first time before the noises began. I gave my gun to Wendy and prepared myself for a sprint through that open spot that was fast approaching ; camera in hand, I was ready!

Then as the thickness ended, and Wendy holding the dogs, I suddenly bolted through the trees and two feet high brush; camera in hand. I was about a hundred feet into this meadow-like patch in the middle of all this brush when I saw some sort of hairy creature, that for a moment, I guessed to be a young bear on its hind legs, disappear behind an old brush and log pile left by forestry workers. I was trying to catch my breath as I ran quietly as possible (while gulping for air); I kept my camera aimed at the pile of brush when there it was; I was starting to see a gorilla, or what in reality I was convinced was a young kid in a Halloween mask, who had been playing a trick the entire time!

So I clicked the camera, figuring this would be a hike to remember, but in that second of thought the face disappeared and I quickly sprinted around the brush pile and there was no kid there. Instead, I was observing some kind of a human-sized, bear-like, brown, hairy animal as it wound among the shorter pine trees and disappeared across the creek and into the forest covered slope of the next mountain. It was not very tall, but it was so fast I couldn't find it again in my viewfinder, and that's when I realized that I had been eyeball to eyeball with a Sasquatch!

Evidently I had shouted something at it out of shock or excitement without even realizing it, because we I got back to the trail Wendy asked me who I was yelling at. When I told her about my experience, she said she heard me yell and then some kind of shriek-like sound from further to her right, which we attributed to the animal, because I didn't even remember hearing it. She had also heard a few thuds, like fast footsteps, but from where she was she couldn't see anything.

I was really excited about this experience, but when I examined the photo on the computer screen at home, the gorilla face didn't come out, and all the image shows is the oblong shape of its head, and where the eyes were so prominent with a reddish tint; there are only two white dots.

As we began to meet more and more hikers and gold miners (yes, they are still out there; we have met many people who are currently living and mining in the Southern Oregon mountains), we have enjoyed conversing with a great number of people in the mining community who have seen and had encounters with Sasquatch, but not only do they wish to remain anonymous, they made us promise to never betray their confidences, on which we gave our word. We value their contributions and honor our commitment, with thanks and admiration for their ability to maintain their lifestyle so secluded and unbeknownst to most residents of Oregon.

Strangely as we were preparing our hiking book, I put this experience aside with doubtful consideration, and then we began meeting and corresponding with more and more people who have had close contacts with Bigfoot. It was then we began paying serious attention to the Sasquatch and indicated our interest in bringing those stories to the light. Our contributor list grew until we had published more books, and the more stories we received, the more I kept thinking back to that Briggs Creek incident.

As I mentioned in the first part of this story, I went back and perused our photo record of this incident and while looking at the shots in color, I finally concluded that I actually did have an encounter with a Sasquatch. Now I am able to believe my own experience was the real thing!

Gary Swanson ~ Southern Utah

ABOUT THE AUTHORS

Gary and Wendy Swanson lived in Grants Pass, Oregon for eight years, where they enjoyed hiking throughout the spring, summer and fall months with their dogs. In addition to their love of hiking, they also enjoy history. Southern Oregon is full of history of gold mining, logging and fishing along the wild and scenic Rogue River; so for them, it has been a great place to research history, explore the countryside and hike all at the same time.

Although they have relocated to sunny Southern Utah, they still enjoy hiking with their miniature schnauzers, and as more Sasquatch stories keep arriving, they have begun to receive some very guarded and secretive information about an almost unbelievably evil creature called "Skinwalker." They are understandably leery of this research, because where Sasquatch is really interesting, the Skinwalker seems disgusting and dangerous. They received many stories of this very evil creature and published them in "Skinwalkers, Shapeshifters and Native American Curses."

If you have had a sighting or an encounter with Sasquatch, or even a Skinwalker, and would like your story published, the Swanson's welcome you to send your contact information, details of the encounter and any photos to swanliterary@gmail.com.